LOUISIANA CEMETERY CASE LAW

This book is a guide for interested notaries, attorneys, funeral directors, church officials, and cemetery directors. It is not legal advice nor the practice of law. The author draws on his practical experience in the field as a cemetery director and as a commissioned Louisiana Civil Law Notary Public, but does not hold himself out to be an attorney at law. Those using any suggestions and forms are advised to confirm and update them with their own research. Use of this book constitutes full and voluntary acceptance of the risk of error, misapplication, or invalidity.

Any statement of "should" or "is advised" or similar is based on the author's personal and practical experience. It is not legal advice.

LOUISIANA CEMETERY CASE LAW

Jurisprudence, Practical Lessons, and Title 8 in the Courts

A Guide to Judicial Interpretation of Cemetery Law, Family Rights, and Sacred Trusts

JOSHUA R. LEBLANC

Bayou State
PUBLISHING

For permission requests, contact:
Bayou State Publishing
P.O. Box 1049
Abbeville, LA 70511
Email: info@bayoustatepublishing.com
Website: bayoustatepublishing.com

ISBN: 978-1-970659-04-7

Printed in the United States of America
First Edition, 2025

Published by **Bayou State Publishing**
Youngsville, LA

Disclaimer:
The information contained in this book is provided for general educational and informational purposes only. Nothing in this book should be construed as, or relied upon as, legal advice. Laws and regulations vary by jurisdiction and are subject to change. Readers are strongly encouraged to consult with a qualified attorney before making any decisions or taking any action based on the material presented herein. The author and publisher expressly disclaim any liability for actions taken or not taken based on the contents of this book.

ABOUT THE AUTHOR

Joshua R. LeBlanc serves as the Executive Director of Holy Family Cemetery in New Iberia, Louisiana. He was ordained a Catholic deacon for the Diocese of Lafayette in 2016 and is currently assigned to St. Martin de Tours Catholic Church in St. Martinville.

Deacon LeBlanc brings a unique combination of theological insight, pastoral care, and administrative precision to the sacred work of cemetery management.

He holds a Master of Arts in Moral Theology and a +30 in Bioethics from Holy Apostles College and Seminary and is certified in Bioethics by the National Catholic Bioethics Center. He is currently pursuing a Doctorate in the field of Bioethics.

In addition to his ministry and administrative leadership, Deacon LeBlanc is a commissioned Civil Law Notary Public in and for the State of Louisiana and the owner of two small businesses – an IT firm and Chesterton's Fine Cigars in Youngsville, La. It is through this background that he shares his expertise in faith, ethics, and cemetery law.

Deacon LeBlanc also serves as a police chaplain and reserve police officer for the Youngsville and Abbeville Police Departments. He is also chaplain for the Military and Hospitaller Order of St. Lazarus of Jerusalem in the rank of Ecclesiastical Commander, whose mission is to serve the sick and dying. He is the Delegate for the Imperial Calcasieu Delegation and Vice Chancellor for Communications for the Grand Priory of America

As a deacon, he has ministered to grieving families for years, guiding them through the Catholic Church's teachings on death, burial, and resurrection. As a professional cemetery administrator, he has developed robust compliance systems rooted in Louisiana law, ensuring that every interment, fund, and record upholds both the dignity of the deceased and the legal obligations of the living.

Deacon LeBlanc is the author of *The Louisiana Cemetery Form Book: Legal Documents, Templates, and Compliance Tools for Cemetery Authorities and Notaries Public*, the companion book in this series. Together, these works form the foundation of *The Louisiana Cemetery Authority Series*, a comprehensive legal and operational reference for religious and civil cemetery professionals throughout the state.

He and his wife, Annie, reside in Abbeville, Louisiana, with their cat Benedict.

THE LOUISIANA CEMETERY AUTHORITY SERIES

The Louisiana Cemetery Handbook: Law, Compliance, and Administration: A comprehensive guide to Louisiana cemetery law, Title 8 statutes, case law, and regulatory compliance.

The Louisiana Cemetery Forms Book: Documents, Templates, and Compliance Tools for Cemetery Authorities and Notaries Public. A companion volume containing practical forms, sample contracts, affidavits, and checklists for daily operations.

Catholic and Cultural Burial Traditions in Louisiana: A Guide to Faith, Heritage, and Sacred Practice. A comprehensive exploration of Louisiana's Catholic, Cajun, Creole, African American, and Native burial customs, offering theological insight, cultural history, and practical guidance for cemetery professionals and families.

Louisiana Cemetery Case Law: Jurisprudence, Practical Lessons, and Title 8 in the Courts. A clear and practical guide to Louisiana's major cemetery cases, this volume explains how courts interpret Title 8 in real-world disputes involving burial authority, disinterment, family cemeteries, undeveloped land sales, trust funds, and historic burial protections.

The Notary's Guide to Louisiana Cemetery Law: Authority, Documentation, and Practice Under Title 8. A practical reference that equips Louisiana notaries with clear, compliant language, clauses, and pastoral guidance for navigating cemetery ownership, interment rights, and Title 8 obligations in everyday notarial practice.

THE LOUISIANA CEMETERY HANDBOOK

Law, Compliance, and Administration

The *Louisiana Cemetery Handbook* is the state's most comprehensive and authoritative guide to the legal, historical, and operational foundations of cemetery management in Louisiana. Written for cemetery authorities, notaries public, attorneys, clergy, and municipal officials, it explains—in clear and practical language—**how Louisiana's unique burial laws work** and how they should be applied in everyday cemetery operations.

This essential volume includes:

- **A full explanation of Louisiana's cemetery laws**, including Title 8, Louisiana Civil Code, and relevant Administrative Code provisions.
- **Historical and cultural background** that illuminates why Louisiana's cemetery laws are distinct from those of any other state.
- **Detailed commentary on interment rights, perpetual care, abandonment procedures, dedication and removal, disinterment, merchandise trust laws, succession issues, and more.**
- **Best-practice guidelines** for cemetery operations, recordkeeping, trust fund compliance, and consumer protection.
- **Practical examples, case studies, and diagrams** to help cemetery personnel apply the law correctly.
- **Professional insights** informed by the author's experience in cemetery administration, notarial practice, and pastoral ministry.

PREFACE

Cemetery law is among the most unusual and emotionally complex areas of Louisiana jurisprudence. It sits at the crossroads of property, family, culture, theology, consumer protection, and public administration. Yet for all its complexity, this area of law is profoundly human. Every legal question that arises – from who may authorize a burial to who may be buried in a family tomb – is rooted in the most fundamental realities of life and death, love and loss, memory and identity.

For years, Cemetery Authorities, notaries, clergy, attorneys, and municipal officials have asked for a unified resource that gathers Louisiana's cemetery case law into a clear, accessible, and practical guide. While the statutes in Title 8 establish the legal structure for cemetery operations, **it is the jurisprudence – the stories of real families and real conflicts – that illuminates how these laws work in practice.** Louisiana's courts have shaped cemetery law with exceptional care, balancing deep respect for the dignity of the deceased with compassion for the living and oversight for those entrusted with cemetery stewardship.

This book was written to meet that need.

The Louisiana Cemetery Authority Series is designed to offer practical tools rooted in legal accuracy, pastoral sensitivity, and administrative clarity. The first volumes focused on statutory interpretation and on providing the forms and templates necessary for day-to-day operations. This volume turns to the courts – to the decisions that define the boundaries of authority, clarify ambiguities in the law, and teach us how to prevent disputes before they begin.

As I worked through the case law, I was struck by the constancy of the themes that appear across decades of litigation: the importance of documentation; the imperative of transparency; the need to respect the statutory hierarchy for burial decisions; the permanent nature of interment; the emotional vulnerability of families; and the sacredness of the spaces we care for. Whether the dispute involved disinterment, family burial grounds, undeveloped land, trust funds, or historic cemeteries, the courts repeatedly affirmed an underlying truth: **cemetery law is a ministry as much as it is a regulatory framework.**

This volume aims to serve both purposes.

It synthesizes Louisiana's cemetery jurisprudence into a structured guide that can be used in training, policy development, administrative decision-making, and professional education. It provides the reasoning behind major decisions, the statutory principles they interpret, and the practical lessons Cemetery Authorities can apply immediately. It also shines a light on the human stories that give these cases their weight — stories of grief, conflict, reconciliation, injustice, and devotion.

My hope is that this book will give Cemetery Authorities, notaries, clergy, and attorneys not only greater legal clarity but also greater confidence in the work they do each day. By understanding how the courts interpret the law, we can prevent misunderstandings, resolve disputes with compassion, and ensure that Louisiana's sacred burial traditions are upheld with the integrity they deserve.

Cemeteries are places of memory, identity, and faith. They are the quiet foundations upon which families and communities are built. Those who serve in cemetery administration carry a responsibility of permanence — a responsibility that endures long after families have dispersed and generations have passed. My prayer is that this volume, like the others in the Louisiana Cemetery Authority Series, will equip you to carry that responsibility with clarity, precision, and reverence.

TABLE OF CONTENTS

INTRODUCTION

Cemeteries occupy a unique and deeply personal place in Louisiana life. They are quiet spaces where law, culture, family, and faith meet – often harmoniously, sometimes with great conflict. Every cemetery, whether a bustling perpetual care memorial park or a rural family plot tucked behind an oak grove, holds within its boundaries the full tapestry of human experience: devotion and grief, family pride and family dysfunction, careful planning and unexpected tragedy. For those who steward these spaces – Cemetery Authorities, notaries, attorneys, clergy, and municipal officials – the responsibility is far more than administrative. It is sacred. It is legal. And it is permanent.

This book exists to help those stewards understand one of the most powerful tools they possess: **Louisiana cemetery jurisprudence** – the body of court decisions that interprets, clarifies, and occasionally reshapes the meaning of Title 8 of the Louisiana Revised Statutes.

Louisiana's cemetery laws are among the most specialized in the United States. Our civil law heritage, Catholic burial traditions, strong family structures, and cultural diversity created a legal landscape unlike that of any other state. Yet the statutes alone do not tell the whole story. It is only through the decisions of Louisiana's courts – from the Supreme Court down to the appellate level – that the true contours of cemetery law emerge. These decisions illustrate how the statutes function in real-life situations: disputes between second spouses and adult children, fights over disinterment, conflicts over ownership of family tombs, problems with cemetery sales and trust funds, and the protection of historic or unmarked burial sites.

In every case, a principle becomes clear: **cemetery law is not theoretical. It is lived. It is emotional. And it is permanent.**

This introduction explains why cemetery jurisprudence matters, how this book is organized, and how the chapters that follow can serve as both a practical guide and a deeper reflection on the duties of those who care for the dead.

Why Cemetery Case Law Matters

Most Louisiana cemeteries operate daily without ever setting foot in a courtroom. Yet nearly every administrative decision — every burial authorization, every interment-right transfer, every trust-fund deposit, every family mediation — occurs within the shadow and guidance of case law.

Jurisprudence matters because:

1. Statutes cannot predict every human conflict.

Title 8 provides rules, but people provide variables: blended families, estranged relationships, long-lost heirs, contested marriages, unclear documentation, and disagreements that erupt when grief and history collide.

The courts fill these gaps.

2. Case law protects families from abuse and misunderstanding.

Decisions like *Giles* safeguard purchasers from false promises about undeveloped cemetery sections. *Sonnier* continues to protect families from wrongful burial decisions. *Begnaud* ensures that cherished family burial grounds remain protected regardless of who owns the surrounding property.

3. Case law protects Cemetery Authorities from liability.

A cemetery with proper documentation, clear policies, and knowledge of jurisprudence is shielded from unnecessary lawsuits. The lessons of *Spiess, Pittman, Westlawn,* and *Gilmore* show cemeteries exactly how to avoid becoming a defendant in a costly dispute.

4. Case law guides professional ethics.

Notaries, funeral directors, clergy, and attorneys rely on jurisprudence to ensure every burial decision is lawful, pastoral, and respectful.

5. Case law forms the foundation for legislative reform.

When statutes are unclear or outdated, jurisprudence points the way to needed improvements in Title 8. This is especially true today as cremation, blended families, environmental pressures, and cultural preservation reshape burial practices.

Simply put: **Cemetery case law is the living interpretation of the duties Louisiana places upon those who care for the dead.**

Why This Book Is Needed

Although Louisiana has a robust statutory framework for cemetery regulation, **no single volume has previously gathered, explained, and**

analyzed the whole body of Louisiana cemetery case law. Professionals had to search across dozens of appellate decisions, often reading through years of litigation to understand a single principle.

This book fills that gap by providing:

- A comprehensive survey of landmark cases
- Clear summaries of holdings and legal principles
- Explanations of how courts interpret statutes
- Practical checklists and model clauses drawn directly from jurisprudence
- Guidance for Cemetery Authorities, notaries, attorneys, clergy, and municipal officials
- Legislative insights for future reform
- A synthesis of historical, cultural, and administrative perspectives

In short, it provides the foundation for confidently and compassionately applying the law in everyday cemetery administration.

How This Book Is Organized

The chapters in this volume follow a deliberate progression from the personal to the structural, from individual burial decisions to statewide regulatory oversight.

Chapters 1–3: Foundations of Cemetery Jurisprudence

These chapters explore the core concepts that shape every burial decision: the nature of interment rights, the distinction between ownership and authority, and the hierarchy of decision-makers under **La. R.S. 8:655**.

Cases like *Sonnier* and *Sobolak* provide grounding for the right of disposition — the heart of burial law.

Chapters 4–7: Disinterment, Family Conflict & Burial Rights

Disinterment cases (*Spiess, Pittman*), burial-authorization disputes, and ownership complications reveal how courts resolve deeply emotional conflicts. *Begnaud* offers a full treatment of family burial grounds — a category unique to Louisiana's cultural heritage.

Chapters 8–9: Sales, Trust Funds & Regulatory Oversight

Cemetery operations intersect with consumer protection and fiduciary duties. *Giles* exposes the risks of selling undeveloped land, while *Westlawn* defines constitutional limits on the Louisiana Cemetery Board.

Chapters 10–11: Historic, Unmarked & Archaeological Burials

These chapters explore the intersection of cemetery law with historic preservation, archaeology, and public policy. The cases surrounding *Christ Church* and *Touro Synagogue*, along with the statutory protections of **La. R.S. 8:671–681** and **La. R.S. 25:931–943**, highlight the reverence owed to older and unmarked sites.

Chapters 12–13: Practical Application & Professional Tools

These chapters convert jurisprudence into daily practice with model forms, recommended clauses, and litigation checklists.

Chapter 14: Future Directions

The concluding chapter looks to the future, identifying areas where modern challenges – blended families, cremation, environmental burial innovation, family cemetery stewardship, and archaeological discoveries – call for thoughtful legislative refinement.

Together, these chapters form a coherent guide for navigating the complexities of Louisiana cemetery law with clarity, confidence, and compassion.

THE HUMAN DIMENSION OF CEMETERY LAW

Every cemetery case originates with a human story.

- A widow seeking to correct a past hurt.
- Siblings disputing the restoration of a parent's tomb.
- A family deceived by promises of a garden that never existed.
- A rural landowner discovering unmarked graves on inherited property.
- A cemetery board attempting to enforce regulations beyond statutory limits.
- A community fighting to preserve a historic burial ground threatened by development.

These stories remind us that cemetery law is not merely transactional. It is relational. It is pastoral. It is sacred.

The courts understand this. Their decisions bear the language of respect and caution – language rarely seen in ordinary property or contract disputes. Judges speak of "the dignity of the human person," "respect for the dead," and "the emotional weight carried by survivors." They recognize that burial places represent permanence in a world of constant change.

This book is written in that same spirit.

THE DUTY OF CEMETERY STEWARDS

Cemetery Authorities, funeral directors, clergy, and notaries are not merely administrators. They are guardians of sacred trust. Their daily actions — the signatures they obtain, the records they preserve, the families they guide — carry legal weight and emotional weight in equal measure.

Jurisprudence teaches that:

- **Documentation preserves peace.**
- **Transparency builds trust.**
- **Equity protects families.**
- **Compliance protects the cemetery.**
- **Respect for tradition preserves heritage.**
- **Understanding the law prevents harm before it begins.**

By studying the cases that shaped Title 8, cemetery stewards gain the wisdom needed to prevent disputes before they arise, resolve conflicts with compassion, and administer their responsibilities with the highest standard of care.

A FINAL WORD ON THE PURPOSE OF THIS BOOK

The purpose of this book is not simply to explain cases. It is to provide Louisiana with a comprehensive, practical, and compassionate guide for administering cemeteries in a way that honors the law, protects families, and upholds the dignity of the dead.

It is written for those who stand daily at the crossroads of grief and governance — those entrusted with the sacred responsibility of caring for the living by caring for the dead.

If this volume strengthens your work, supports your ministry, or deepens your understanding of the law's role in cemetery stewardship, then it has succeeded in its purpose.

CHAPTER 1

WHY CEMETERY CASE LAW MATTERS

Cemeteries occupy a uniquely sacred and legally complex space in Louisiana. They are places of burial and prayer, but also regulated entities grounded in civil law, statutory duties, and trust obligations. Because of this dual nature, disputes over burial, disinterment, consumer protection, ownership of cemetery spaces, and the administration of perpetual care funds often end up in court. When they do, judges must interpret Title 8, the Civil Code, the Louisiana Constitution, and sometimes federal law – and their decisions form an essential body of cemetery jurisprudence.

For Cemetery Authorities, attorneys, notaries public, and even clergy, understanding these cases is not optional. Case law clarifies statutes, resolves ambiguities, and tests real-world scenarios. It is where we see how courts balance competing family claims, how far Cemetery Authorities may go in enforcing rules, and what remedies exist when a cemetery project fails, a family quarrel erupts, or remains must be moved.

Louisiana's Civil-Law Foundation

Other than Puerto Rico, Louisiana is the only civil law jurisdiction in the United States. Statutes are the primary source of law, and jurisprudence plays a persuasive – but not formally binding – role. Yet, in practice, Louisiana courts rely heavily on prior decisions when interpreting Title 8, especially in emotionally charged areas such as disinterment and the right of disposition. When a dispute arises, attorneys and judges invariably cite the same cluster of cases: **Sonnier, Spiess, Pittman, Begnaud, Giles, Westlawn,** and the historic expropriation cases involving Girod Street Cemetery.

These cases form a practical roadmap. They illustrate how statutory language operates when applied to fractured families, uncooperative cemetery operators, defaulting purchasers, or public entities navigating abandoned burial grounds.

Why Case Law Matters for Cemetery Authorities

For Cemetery Authorities, jurisprudence is not academic. It directly affects:

- **Internal Policies.** Disinterment procedures must reflect *Spiess* and *Sonnier*. Board-adopted policies should mirror the hierarchy of consent in **La. R.S. 8:655** and the "abuse-of-discretion" standard applied by appellate courts.
- **Contracting Practices.** Cases like **Giles v. Oak Lane** reveal risks in selling undeveloped land, family garden projects, and misleading representations. The lessons from these decisions help shape compliant purchase agreements.
- **Trust Administration. Westlawn v. Louisiana Cemetery Board** sets constitutional limits on LCB rulemaking and reminds cemetery owners that trust compliance is not merely regulatory – it has constitutional and judicial implications as well.
- **Recordkeeping and Liability.** Courts consistently look to written records when determining ownership of plots, consent

for burial, and authority for disinterment. A single missing contract or misfiled declaration can shift an entire case.

WHY CASE LAW MATTERS FOR FAMILIES & CLERGY

Families rarely expect to navigate the legal system when burying their loved ones. But disputes arise – between divorced parents, estranged siblings, surviving spouses, and blended families. Clergy, funeral directors, and notaries are often caught in the middle.

Understanding the jurisprudence equips them to:

- advise grieving families correctly,
- prevent unintended litigation,
- recognize when competing claims require legal resolution, and
- ensure that both pastoral and legal duties are fulfilled.

Cases like **Sobolak v. Sobolak (2025)** show how quickly burial disputes escalate when parents disagree. The jurisprudence reinforces the pastoral principle: clarity prevents conflict.

THE ROLE OF CASE LAW IN LEGISLATIVE INTERPRETATION

Louisiana's cemetery statutes evolved significantly in 1974, 1990, 2008, and 2018–2022. Courts commonly examine the legislative history behind these amendments – often citing **Matter of Dufour (1993)** – to interpret the rights to control interment, to exercise disinterment authority, and to obtain family-burial-ground status. Understanding this history is essential for correctly applying current law.

When courts interpret statutes inconsistently, the Legislature often responds. Future Title 8 revisions will almost certainly react to cases like *Westlawn, Giles,* and *Sonnier.*

PURPOSE OF THIS BOOK

This volume gathers the most significant Louisiana cemetery cases and explains them in a clear, practical way. Each chapter:

- summarizes the case in readable prose,
- contextualizes the statutory issues,
- identifies the rule or principle the case established,
- outlines the practical implications for Cemetery Authorities, notaries, attorneys, and families, and
- provides forms, checklists, or policy guidance where appropriate.

The goal is not merely academic analysis but a **usable tool** for anyone working in Louisiana cemetery administration or advising families during times of loss.

Jurisprudence shapes the living memory of Title 8. Through these cases, we learn how Louisiana courts protect the dignity of the dead, the rights of families, and the responsibilities of those entrusted with sacred land.

CHAPTER 2

READING CEMETERY CASES: STANDARDS OF REVIEW & JUDICIAL METHOD

Cemetery disputes occupy a small but deeply consequential section of Louisiana jurisprudence. Because they arise at the intersection of statutory interpretation, family law, property law, trust law, and pastoral concerns, courts often navigate these cases with a heightened sense of care. To understand any cemetery decision – and to apply that decision correctly – the reader must understand how Louisiana courts structure their analysis. This chapter explains the tools courts use and the reasoning patterns that appear repeatedly in cemetery opinions.

THE ANATOMY OF A LOUISIANA APPELLATE OPINION

Every Louisiana appellate decision follows a recognizable framework. Appreciating this structure helps practitioners identify where the court is making findings of fact, interpreting statutes, or engaging in policy reasoning.

1. **Facts and Procedural History**
   The court recounts the facts and the path the case took to reach the appellate court.

Example: In *Sonnier*, the Third Circuit described the plot ownership dispute, the burial of the decedent, the filing of the petition for disinterment, and the trial court's denial before reviewing the matter.

2. **Assignments of Error / Issues Presented**
   The court identifies the legal questions. For cemetery cases, the typical issues include:
   - Who has the right to control interment under **La. R.S. 8:655**?
   - Under what circumstances may remains be moved under **La. R.S. 8:659**?
   - Does **La. R.S. 8:658** limit the type of action brought?
   - Did the Cemetery Authority comply with trust requirements?
   - Was cemetery land legally abandoned, expropriated, or sold?
3. **Standard of Review**
   This determines the level of deference to the trial court. Standards of review matter enormously in cemetery cases, because they often determine whether the appellate court even reaches the merits.
4. **Law and Analysis**
   Courts interpret statutes, reference prior cases, and apply the law to the facts.
5. **Holding and Decree**
   The court's formal ruling — affirming, reversing, modifying, or remanding.

Understanding this structure helps the practitioner extract the "rule" from the opinion and apply it to cemetery administration or litigation.

Standards of Review in Cemetery Cases

Louisiana appellate courts use several standards of review, but two dominate cemetery litigation: **abuse of discretion** and **de novo** review.

Abuse of Discretion: The Core Standard for Disinterment

When determining whether remains may be disinterred under **La. R.S. 8:659**, appellate courts consistently apply an **abuse-of-discretion** standard.

This means:

- The trial judge's decision stands **unless** it was arbitrary, unreasonable, or unsupported by the evidence.
- Appellate courts do **not** reweigh the emotional equities or substitute their own judgment simply because they might have reached a different result.

This standard originates in cases like **Spiess v. Greenwood Development Co. (1989)** and is reaffirmed in **Pittman v. Magic City Memorial Co. (2008)** and the *Sonnier* line of cases. Courts emphasize that trial judges are best positioned to hear sensitive testimony and evaluate the impact of moving remains.

Practical consequence:
If a Cemetery Authority or family member is litigating a disinterment request, the *battle is usually won or lost in the trial court.*

De Novo Review: Statutory Interpretation and Legal Questions

When a case turns on the interpretation of Title 8, such as the meaning of "surviving spouse," the application of the family hierarchy in **La. R.S. 8:655**, or the scope of the Louisiana Cemetery Board's rulemaking authority, courts apply **de novo** review.

This means the appellate court gives **no deference** to the trial court's legal interpretation.

Examples:

- **Westlawn v. Louisiana Cemetery Board** involved de novo review to determine whether the Board exceeded statutory authority in requiring additional perpetual care trust deposits.
- **Gilmore v. Whited** applied de novo review to clarify the limits of **La. R.S. 8:658.**
- Portions of **Sonnier** also applied de novo review when determining the interaction between PADD designations and the statutory right of disposition.

Practical consequence:
Legal arguments rooted in statutory interpretation carry full force at the appellate level, even if the trial court ruled differently.

How Louisiana Courts Interpret Title 8

Louisiana courts follow clear interpretive rules:

Plain Meaning First

Courts begin with the text. If La. R.S. 8:655 or 8:659 is unambiguous, the inquiry ends. This principle frequently appears in disinterment decisions: if the statute creates a hierarchy of decision-makers, courts apply it strictly.

Harmonizing Related Statutes

Courts strive to read sections of Title 8 together so that none are rendered meaningless.

This is important when interpreting:

- **La. R.S. 8:655** (interment authority)
- **La. R.S. 8:659** (disinterment authority)
- **La. R.S. 8:660** (Cemetery Authority's independent role)

Key cases emphasize that the right to decide **where someone is initially buried** is not the same as the right to later **move** that person – a distinction central to *Spiess* and *Sonnier*.

Legislative Purpose & Historical Context

When the law is ambiguous, courts examine the purpose behind the statute. For example:

- *Matter of Dufour (1993)* looked at the 1990 amendments that rewrote the right-of-disposition statutes.
- *Giles v. Oak Lane* relied on legislative history regarding the sale of cemetery spaces on undeveloped land.

AVOIDING ABSURD OR UNJUST RESULTS

Cemetery cases often involve emotional or pastoral concerns. Courts sometimes invoke equity principles to avoid interpretations that would produce unreasonable outcomes, though they do so cautiously.

Example: Courts avoid interpretations of **La. R.S. 8:655** that would allow a distant relative to override a more invested family member simply because of technical priority.

EXTRACTING THE "RULE" FROM A CEMETERY CASE

Each appellate opinion leaves the practitioner with a distilled rule. Examples we'll explore later include:

- **"The decision to disinter remains is reviewed for abuse of discretion."** (Spiess, Pittman)
- **"The PADD designation affects military disposition but not Louisiana civilian disinterment."** (Sonnier)
- **"La. R.S. 8:658 applies only to actions against Cemetery Authorities, not private individuals."** (Gilmore)
- **"The Cemetery Board cannot regulate beyond the authority expressly granted in Title 8."** (Westlawn)
- **"A family burial ground exists by statute even if not formally established by deed."** (Begnaud)

Once these rules are identified, they can be transformed into operational policies, notary templates, burial declarations, and cemetery board procedures.

Why Standards of Review Matter for Practitioners

If a Cemetery Authority or family is considering litigation, understanding the applicable standard of review helps assess the likelihood of success:

- **Abuse of discretion** → limited chance of reversal.
- **De novo review** → strong opportunity to challenge an incorrect legal conclusion.

For attorneys and notaries, this means identifying early whether the dispute is **fact-driven** (discretion) or **law-driven** (statutory interpretation).

For Cemetery Authorities, this informs which decisions must be documented meticulously (e.g., consent for disinterment) and which policies must be drafted with statutory precision (e.g., trusting practices after *Westlawn*).

Conclusion

Reading and applying cemetery case law requires more than scanning the holding. The practitioner must understand how courts reason, which standards of review govern the dispute, and how Title 8 interacts with broader areas of Louisiana law. Equipped with this framework, the reader is prepared to enter the heart of this volume – the landmark cases that define the contours of Louisiana cemetery practice.

WHY STANDARDS OF REVIEW MATTER FOR PRACTITIONERS

CHAPTER 3

THE RIGHT OF DISPOSITION UNDER LA. R.S. 8:655

The right to control the disposition of human remains – known in Common law as right of sepulcher, but in Louisiana law as the **right of disposition** – lies at the heart of nearly every cemetery dispute. Louisiana treats burial not merely as a cultural or religious act, but as a legal event governed by statute. **La. R.S. 8:655** establishes a strict hierarchy of persons who may determine the place and manner of disposition, and Louisiana courts have repeatedly emphasized that this hierarchy is to be applied as written. Yet, as the jurisprudence shows, real cases rarely fit neatly into the statute's clean lines.

This chapter explains the structure of the right of disposition, the meaning of the statutory hierarchy, and the lessons drawn from Louisiana's most significant right-of-disposition cases – with *Sonnier, Sobolak,* and *Dufour* providing the backbone of modern interpretation.

THE LEGAL FRAMEWORK OF LA. R.S. 8:655

Louisiana's right-of-disposition statute creates an ordered list of individuals empowered to make decisions regarding the "disposition of remains." The intent is clarity: in moments of grief, the law supplies a default structure so families and Cemetery Authorities are not left in paralysis or conflict.

The statutory order begins with any written, notarized declaration executed by the decedent. If none exists, the hierarchy proceeds to the surviving spouse, then to the adult children, then to the parents, siblings, and so forth. Each class must act collectively unless the statute expressly indicates otherwise.

Courts interpret this statute strictly. The hierarchy is not advisory. A family member with lower priority may not override one with higher priority merely because of a stronger emotional bond or a closer relationship.

However, this clarity is often complicated by divorce decrees, estrangements, stepfamilies, military designations, and questions of mental capacity – all of which appear throughout Louisiana jurisprudence.

Lessons from Sonnier: When Statutes and Military Designations Collide

The seminal case of *Sonnier v. Catholic Foundation of the Diocese of Lafayette* brought national attention to the right of disposition. In *Sonnier*, the decedent had a military PADD designation and a DD Form 93 naming a particular individual to control disposition for military purposes. However, Louisiana's statute – not federal military paperwork – governed the civilian interment decision.

The Louisiana Supreme Court's ruling clarified two essential principles:

- A PADD or DD Form 93 controls only the **initial disposition of remains while in military custody**, not civilian disinterment or later disputes in Louisiana courts.
- Once the remains are returned to civilian authority, **La. R.S. 8:655 controls exclusively**.

This ruling reshaped how funeral directors, notaries, and Cemetery Authorities interpret military documentation. It also confirmed that even well-intended designations cannot supersede Louisiana's statutory hierarchy once the decedent is home.

The Sonnier Line of Cases and the Importance of Written Declarations

The multiple appellate decisions flowing from the *Sonnier* litigation further established that written declarations executed by the decedent – if notarized and compliant with statute – stand at the top of the hierarchy. Courts will enforce such declarations even in the face of strong family objections.

For practitioners, the lesson is unambiguous:

- Encourage individuals to execute **written burial declarations** before death.
- Ensure that such declarations are notarized and clearly state the decedent's wishes.
- Store these declarations in permanent cemetery files to prevent later disputes.

Families often believe their verbal wishes will be respected. *Sonnier* makes clear: documentation is everything.

Disputes Between Parents: Guidance from Sobolak

In 2025, the Second Circuit issued *Sobolak v. Sobolak*, a highly instructive case involving divorced parents who disagreed about their child's burial location. The court applied **La. R.S. 8:655(A)(5)**, which places "the surviving parents" at the same hierarchical level.

The holding reinforced two important rules:

- When a class consists of more than one person – such as parents or children – **the majority must agree**. This effectively means that, in the case of parents, both must agree.
- Disagreement among equal-priority decision-makers prevents either from taking unilateral action.

In *Sobolak*, neither parent could independently choose the burial site. The court emphasized the need for cooperative decision-making or judicial intervention.

For Cemetery Authorities, this case highlights the need to:

- Request signatures from **both** parents when the statute places them in the same category.
- Document all consent and communication.
- Decline to proceed when competing claims exist without a court order.

Interment Rights vs. Burial Authority

A recurring misunderstanding in cemetery disputes is the assumption that **ownership of interment rights confers authority to decide who is buried there.** Louisiana courts have firmly rejected this idea.

Ownership of burial rights is a **property interest.**

The right to control disposition is a **personal status interest** governed by statute.

Key cases — including appellate rulings in the *Sonnier* litigation — repeatedly clarify that a person may own a tomb yet have zero authority over the remains placed within it. Conversely, a person may have authority to control disposition even when they own no cemetery burial rights at all.

This distinction is critical for notaries and Cemetery Authorities drafting:

- transfer forms,
- declarations of interment rights,
- burial agreements, and
- family-ownership affidavits.

The Role of Legislative History: Insights from Dufour

The Matter of Dufour remains one of the most instructive early cases interpreting the purpose of Louisiana's revised right-of-disposition law following the 1990 statutory overhaul. The Fourth Circuit examined the Legislature's intent to create:

- a clear hierarchy,
- predictable procedures,
- reduced family conflict, and
- a uniform mechanism for fast, orderly burial decisions.

Courts still rely on *Dufour* when interpreting ambiguities in the statute. It is a reminder that Title 8's right-of-disposition statutes were designed to eliminate confusion — and that courts will interpret them in favor of clarity and hierarchy, not informal preference or emotional argument.

Practical Guidance for Practitioners

Practitioners who regularly encounter cemetery disputes should internalize several principles from these cases:

- Always determine the statutory class and ensure the correct individuals sign the burial or disinterment documents.
- When multiple people occupy the same priority level, obtain **all signatures**.
- Do not rely on PADDs, funeral home worksheets, verbal statements, or electronic messages as substitutes for statutory compliance.
- Encourage families to prepare declarations in advance, especially in blended families, military families, and contentious family situations.
- When in doubt, pause and request a court order rather than risk liability.

Cemetery Authorities must be vigilant. Proceeding with burial or disinterment based on flawed or incomplete consent exposes the cemetery to litigation, reputational harm, and — in particularly egregious situations — possible statutory penalties.

Conclusion

The right of disposition shapes every other area of cemetery management. It determines who can authorize burial, who can challenge decisions, and who can seek judicial relief. Through *Sonnier*, *Sobolak*, *Dufour*, and related cases, Louisiana courts have developed a clear, structured, and enforceable framework for resolving disputes with both legal precision and pastoral sensitivity.

With this foundation in place, we turn next to the most emotionally charged aspect of cemetery practice: the movement of human remains.

CHAPTER 4

MOVING THE DEAD: DISINTERMENT UNDER LA. R.S. 8:655 & 8:666

Of all matters involving cemetery law, none carries greater emotional weight than the movement of human remains. Disinterment disputes test the balance between family wishes, the sanctity of burial, public health concerns, and the authority of cemetery operators. Louisiana law approaches disinterment cautiously, recognizing that the original burial is meant to be permanent, yet acknowledging that circumstances sometimes require relocation.

This chapter examines the statutory framework governing disinterment, the jurisprudence that interprets it, and the standards courts use to evaluate requests to disturb the dead.

THE STATUTORY FRAMEWORK OF LA. R.S. 8:659

La. R.S. 8:659 outlines the requirements for moving remains once they have been interred. The statute requires:

- **written consent of the Cemetery Authority**,
- **written consent of the person(s) with the right to control disposition**, and

- **a court order** when the required consents cannot be obtained.

The statute recognizes that disinterment affects multiple stakeholders – the cemetery as custodian of the remains, the family as holders of the right of disposition, and the court as final arbiter when conflict arises.

The Legislature's intent is plain: disinterment is not a casual event. It is a grave disruption of what should be a final resting place, and strict safeguards must govern it.

The Distinction Between Interment Authority and Disinterment Authority

One of the most important legal insights – established firmly by Louisiana jurisprudence – is that **the authority to inter a body is not the same as the authority to move a body later**.

This distinction first appeared clearly in *Spiess v. Greenwood Development Co. (1989)* and was repeatedly reaffirmed in the *Sonnier* cases. The courts emphasize that:

- A person with the right to decide where someone is **initially buried (La. R.S. 8:655)**
- does **not automatically have the power** to later demand the body be moved.

This principle prevents constant re-litigation of burial decisions and protects the finality of interment. It also prevents lower-priority family members from using disinterment as a tool to undo relationships, revisit past grievances, or exercise control long after the funeral is over.

Lessons from Spiess: The First Major Disinterment Case

Spiess remains the foundational case for understanding disinterment in Louisiana. The Third Circuit held that:

- Disinterment is an **extraordinary remedy**,
- Trial courts have **broad discretion** to grant or deny such requests, and
- Appellate courts review these decisions only for **abuse of discretion.**

The facts of *Spiess* – involving a land-development conflict and attempts to relocate remains – provided the court with a backdrop for articulating enduring policy: burial is intended to be permanent, and any deviation must be supported by compelling justification.

For practitioners, *Spiess* established the framework we still use today:

- The trial court hears testimony, weighs family wishes, and evaluates the circumstances of burial.
- Unless the trial court's conclusion is unreasonable or arbitrary, the appellate courts will not disturb it.

Pittman and the Strength of Trial Court Discretion

Pittman v. Magic City Memorial Co. (2008) reaffirmed the deference given to trial courts in disinterment disputes. In *Pittman,* the appellate court emphasized:

- disinterment decisions require sensitive balancing,
- trial courts are closest to the emotional realities of the parties, and
- appellate intervention is rare.

The case underscores a message for litigants: **if you cannot secure disinterment at the trial level, you are unlikely to succeed on appeal.**

For Cemetery Authorities, *Pittman* shows the importance of keeping thorough records, documenting family consent, and maintaining consistent policies — all of which help trial courts make informed judgments.

The Sonnier Decisions: Disinterment Meets Family Conflict

While *Sonnier* is best known for its interpretation of the right of disposition, its later appellate decisions also address disinterment extensively.

The courts clarified that:

- The person with authority under **La. R.S. 8:655** may give **initial consent** to interment,
- but **disinterment requires additional justification** and is governed separately by **La. R.S. 8:659**,
- and family divisions, second marriages, or unresolved ownership disputes do not automatically justify moving the remains.

In practice, *Sonnier* illustrates the emotional explosion that accompanies many disinterment petitions: arguments over plot ownership, estranged relationships, and even religious preferences.

Yet the courts consistently returned to the statute and the principles first articulated in *Spiess.*

The Role of Cemetery Authorities Under La. R.S. 8:660

Cemetery Authorities are not passive observers in disinterment disputes. **La. R.S. 8:660** grants them independent authority to regulate the manner in which disinterment occurs, including:

- operational procedures,
- safety measures,
- scheduling,
- environmental considerations, and
- compliance with any applicable public health rules.

Although Cemetery Authorities cannot unilaterally override a court order or the consent of the statutory decision-makers, they **can require compliance with reasonable rules** for the protection of cemetery property and personnel.

The courts have recognized this authority as distinct and essential. In cases arising after *Sonnier*, cemetery operators were permitted to impose conditions on disinterment even when the court approved the removal of remains.

Equitable and Pastoral Considerations

Disinterment cases almost always involve grief, unresolved family wounds, or the desire for reconciliation. Courts acknowledge these emotions but remain anchored in legal standards. Judges frequently note that:

- emotional preference alone does not justify disinterment,
- convenience is not a sufficient reason, and
- "second thoughts" by family members do not undo the original interment decision.

Nevertheless, Louisiana courts show compassion in cases where:

- the original burial occurred in error,
- the family was misled,
- a minor child's burial was mishandled, or
- The decedent's express wishes were not honored.

It is here that the law's pastoral dimension intersects with judicial authority: courts attempt to protect both the dignity of the dead and the peace of the living.

Practical Guidance for Cemetery Authorities and Notaries Public

Professionals involved in disinterment should remember several key principles derived from jurisprudence:

- Obtain **written consent** from all persons required by **La. R.S. 8:659.**
- Never proceed with disinterment based on verbal approval.
- Document all communications with family members.
- Follow a written disinterment policy consistent with statute and jurisprudence.
- Require a court order when there is any dispute or uncertainty.
- Preserve all burial and ownership records permanently.

Cemetery Authorities also benefit from consulting legal counsel early, especially when multiple family members are involved, when out-of-state paperwork is presented, or when competing claims arise.

CONCLUSION

Disinterment is a profound and often painful legal process. Louisiana law treats it with the seriousness it deserves, insisting upon strict procedures, explicit consent, and judicial oversight. Through *Spiess*, *Pittman*, and *Sonnier*, the courts have built a consistent and principled approach: burial is meant to be final, and disturbing that finality requires compelling justification.

Having explored the right to inter and the right to disinter, we now turn to a closely related area of conflict — the ownership and inheritance of cemetery spaces.

CHAPTER 5

BURIAL LITIGATION, PRESCRIPTION, AND LA. R.S. 8:658

One of the least understood – and most frequently misapplied – sections of Louisiana cemetery law is **La. R.S. 8:658**, which governs prescription (the Louisiana term for what is known in Common Law as Statute of Limitation), immunity, and the circumstances under which actions may be brought against Cemetery Authorities. Although short, this statute has generated significant litigation, primarily because parties often misunderstand whom it protects, what claims it bars, and how the courts interpret its language.

This chapter explains the scope of **La. R.S. 8:658**, how Louisiana courts have applied it, and what it means for Cemetery Authorities, families, and practitioners.

UNDERSTANDING LA. R.S. 8:658

La. R.S. 8:658 was enacted to provide reasonable protection to Cemetery Authorities and to establish uniformity in the timing of claims involving burial, cemetery operations, and related issues. The statute serves two purposes:

- creating a **time limit** (prescription) for certain actions; and

- granting **limited immunity** to Cemetery Authorities under specific circumstances.

Cemetery operators often believe this statute shields them from most lawsuits. But the jurisprudence shows that the protection is narrower than many assume — and applies only in cases where the defendant meets the statutory definition of a "Cemetery Authority."

In other words, **La. R.S. 8:658 does not grant immunity to private individuals**, even when the dispute involves burial or interment rights.

This principle is central to the leading case interpreting the statute.

Gilmore v. Whited: The Landmark Interpretation

The most important decision concerning **La. R.S. 8:658** is *Gilmore v. Whited*, a First Circuit case that clarified the statute's reach. In *Gilmore*, a dispute arose between individual family members involving the handling of remains and access to a burial site. One party sought to invoke **La. R.S. 8:658** as a defense.

The court rejected the argument.

The First Circuit held:

- **La. R.S. 8:658 applies only to actions against a "Cemetery Authority."**
- The statute does **not** apply to disputes between private persons, heirs, or family members.
- Immunity and prescription under this statute cannot be used as a shield by individuals acting outside the scope of the Cemetery Authority.

This ruling is vital for practitioners because it prevents misuse of statutory protections and ensures families retain remedies against individuals who interfere with burial decisions, disturb remains, or commit acts of fraud or obstruction.

Scope of Immunity Under La. R.S. 8:658

Cemetery Authorities are afforded protection only when they act:

- **in good faith**,
- **within the ordinary course of cemetery operations**, and
- **consistent with written laws or valid authorizations**.

Immunity does **not** cover:

- intentional wrongdoing,
- reckless or grossly negligent conduct,
- violations of trust-fund statutes,
- mismanagement of perpetual care obligations, or
- unauthorized disinterment or burial.

The statute thus protects responsible operators who rely on documentation provided by families, but it does not shield misconduct.

Prescription and Timeliness of Claims

La. R.S. 8:658 also establishes a prescriptive period for various cemetery-related claims. Although often misunderstood, the jurisprudence interprets the statute to require that claims against Cemetery Authorities be brought **within one year** of the act or omission giving rise to the dispute.

However, because cemetery injuries often involve emotional trauma, multiple family members, or long delays in discovering irregularities, courts sometimes analyze:

- when the claimant acquired **actual knowledge** of the potential wrongdoing,
- whether the cemetery concealed relevant information, or
- whether equitable tolling principles apply.

Practitioners should not assume the one-year period is absolute; courts consider the specific facts of each case.

Interaction With Other Statutes

When disputes arise, **La. R.S. 8:658** interacts with related statutes, such as:

- **La. R.S. 8:655** (right of disposition),
- **La. R.S. 8:659** (disinterment),
- **La. R.S. 8:660** (Cemetery Authority responsibilities),
- **La. R.S. 8:802–804** (interment right transfers), and
- **La. R.S. 8:306–308** (perpetual care and merchandise trust violations).

Courts view **La. R.S. 8:658** as a procedural shield, not a substantive override. It does not negate the duties imposed by other Title 8 statutes.

For example:

- A Cemetery Authority cannot cite **La. R.S. 8:658** to excuse selling undeveloped land in violation of **La. R.S. 8:704** or **La. R.S. 8:705.1**.

- Nor can an operator use **La. R.S. 8:658** to justify disinterment actions that violate **La. R.S. 8:659**.

This ensures statutory cohesion across Title 8.

Practical Implications for Cemetery Authorities

Cemetery Authorities should view **La. R.S. 8:658** as a **limited protective tool**, not a blanket defense. The statute offers protection when:

- proper documentation is obtained,
- statutory procedures are followed,
- employees rely reasonably on family paperwork, and
- no bad-faith conduct is involved.

The best protection, however, is **meticulous recordkeeping** and **compliance with statutory requirements**, not reliance on immunity provisions.

Furthermore, because *Gilmore* narrowed the statute's applicability, Cemetery Authorities must be cautious not to assume that families lack recourse simply because Title 8 is implicated.

Practical Implications for Families and Attorneys

For families, *Gilmore* ensures that **La. R.S. 8:658** cannot be used to shield wrongful conduct by private individuals, such as:

- interfering with burial,
- forging consent documents,
- blocking access to cemetery spaces, or
- wrongfully excluding relatives from attending a burial.

Attorneys representing families should investigate:

- whether the defendant is truly a "Cemetery Authority,"
- whether the cemetery acted in good faith,
- whether documentation was properly secured under **La. R.S. 8:655** or **La. R.S. 8:659**, and
- whether prescription has been interrupted by concealment or late discovery.

Proper factual development often determines whether **La. R.S. 8:658** applies at all.

CONCLUSION

La. R.S. 8:658 is a short statute with outsized influence. Through *Gilmore* and related jurisprudence, Louisiana courts have drawn clear boundaries around its protections, preserving fairness while allowing Cemetery Authorities to perform their duties without constant fear of liability.

The statute provides a balance – shielding cemeteries that act responsibly while ensuring families retain meaningful recourse for wrongdoing. When applied correctly, it harmonizes with the broader framework of Title 8 and reinforces the Legislature's intention to promote dignity, order, and accountability in cemetery operations.

With prescription and immunity clarified, the next chapter turns to an equally significant question: who owns the tomb, who inherits interment rights, and how do Louisiana courts resolve conflicts over cemetery property?

CHAPTER 6

OWNERSHIP OF CEMETERY SPACES & INTERMENT RIGHTS

Few areas of cemetery law generate more confusion – or more litigation – than the distinction between **owning** cemetery burial rights and **controlling** who is buried within it. Louisiana law treats cemetery property differently from other immovable property, and misunderstanding this difference often results in bitter family disputes, succession complications, and misinformed claims by heirs.

This chapter explains the nature of cemetery ownership, the legal meaning of interment rights, and the jurisprudence that guides courts when families disagree about who may be buried in a particular space.

OWNERSHIP VS. INTERMENT RIGHTS: A CRUCIAL DISTINCTION

The Louisiana Supreme Court and courts of appeal have made one principle abundantly clear:

Owning burial rights in a space does not give a person the right to decide who is buried in it.

Burial rights ownership is a *real right* tied to immovable property. Control over burial is a *personal right* governed by **La. R.S. 8:655**.

This distinction is central to several major cases, including the *Sonnier* appellate decisions, where the dispute focused partly on who owned adjacent cemetery spaces and partly on who held the statutory authority to make burial decisions. The courts made it clear that ownership alone confers:

- a right to maintain the tomb,
- a right to repair or modify the structure,
- a right to erect markers consistent with cemetery rules, and
- a right of access and use.

But ownership does **not** determine who may be interred.

The Structure of Interment Rights Under Title 8

Louisiana's statutory scheme treats the right of interment as a distinct legal interest separate from property ownership. Various provisions govern these rights:

- The right to control disposition is governed by **La. R.S. 8:655**.
- Disinterment and relocation of remains are governed by **La. R.S. 8:659**.
- Cemetery authority responsibilities are defined in **La. R.S. 8:660**.
- Transfers of interment rights are governed by **La. R.S. 8:802**, **La. R.S. 8:803**, and **La. R.S. 8:804**.

These provisions create a structure in which the Cemetery Authority oversees the physical property, while the right to determine burial is vested in a statutorily defined person or class.

Transfer of Interment Rights: Statutory Requirements

The sale or transfer of interment rights is regulated carefully under Title 8.

The relevant statutes – **La. R.S. 8:802–804** – require:

- written documentation,
- recordation in the cemetery's ownership records,
- compliance with any cemetery rules or dedication documents, and
- acknowledgment and approval by the Cemetery Authority.

A key point for notaries and Cemetery Authorities is that interment rights may be transferred, but ownership of the underlying land always remains with the Cemetery. Individuals often mistakenly believe they are purchasing or inheriting land, whereas they are actually obtaining burial rights on land owned by the Cemetery; therefore, documentation should reflect this fact.

The law thus separates the **metes-and-bounds property interest** from the **right-of-burial functional interest.**

Inheritance of Cemetery Plots: The Begnaud Case

One of the most informative cases on inheritance and family burial grounds is *Succession of Begnaud.* In this case, the Third Circuit examined a privately owned family cemetery located on ancestral land. The court held that the cemetery qualified as a **"family burial ground"** under **La. R.S. 8:1(24).**

The court emphasized that:

- Family burial grounds arise by operation of statute, even if not formally created by deed.
- Heirs inherit the use of such a cemetery regardless of who owns the surrounding property.
- Burial eligibility follows the statutory definition, not the preferences of an individual heir.

This case illustrates how courts treat burial grounds as **quasi-sacred spaces** in which ordinary property rules give way to special statutory protections.

For practitioners, *Begnaud* serves as a template for resolving:

- disputes among heirs about burial eligibility,
- questions of access through private land, and
- conflicts where one heir seeks control over burial decisions.

Burial Rights Ownership Disputes in the Sonnier Litigation

Throughout the various *Sonnier* appellate decisions, family members argued over ownership of burial rights in adjacent cemetery spaces and whether ownership conferred authority to disinter or reinter the decedent.

The courts reaffirmed the guiding principle: **Ownership of burial rights in a cemetery space does not override the statutory hierarchy of La. R.S. 8:655.**

Even if a family member holds title to a space, the person with the higher priority under **La. R.S. 8:655** controls the burial.

This principle protects certainty and prevents plot ownership from becoming a tool for coercion or retaliation.

Interment Rights as Movable or Immovable Property?

Louisiana courts have described interment rights as a "limited real right," but their precise classification can vary depending on context. In general:

- The **land** beneath the cemetery space is immovable and belongs to the cemetery (cemetery retains naked ownership).
- The **right to inter** is treated as a separate right, often transferred by instruments similar to movables regulated by the Cemetery.
- Succession law treats interment rights as **personal rights** rather than full ownership rights because a right to burial is a personal servitude and not an ownership of property.

Practitioners should therefore treat interment rights as **unique hybrid interests** that require:

- clear paperwork,
- cemetery approval, and
- proper recordation.

Access to Family Burial Sites on Private Land

In family cemeteries or rural burial grounds, heirs may need to cross private property to reach graves. Louisiana courts have recognized that:

- inherent in the right to maintain a burial site is the right of **reasonable access**,

- such access may be judicially enforced, and
- the owner of surrounding property may not unreasonably bar descendants.

Although not codified explicitly in Title 8, the concept aligns with longstanding Louisiana public policy and the family cemetery provisions of **La. R.S. 8:1(24)**.

Practical Guidance for Cemetery Authorities, Notaries & Attorneys

Professionals dealing with cemetery property issues should adhere to the following principles:

- Always distinguish clearly between **ownership** and **interment rights**.
- Ensure that transfers under **La. R.S. 8:802–804** are properly documented, approved, and recorded by the Cemetery Authority.
- Advise families that burial decisions follow **La. R.S. 8:655**, not ownership interests.
- Require evidence of authority before allowing burial in a space owned by someone other than the statutory decision-maker.
- Retain detailed records to prevent future litigation.
- Encourage families to execute declarations of interment rights, especially in blended-family contexts.
- When disputes arise, require a judicial order rather than proceed based on informal agreements or assumptions.

Cemetery Authorities should also ensure that their own rules clearly articulate the difference between ownership and burial authority, thereby preventing family disputes from escalating into litigation.

CONCLUSION

Ownership of cemetery spaces is a deeply emotional and legally nuanced matter. Louisiana courts have carved out a consistent doctrine: ownership does not confer burial authority, and burial authority does not imply property ownership. Through cases like *Begnaud* and *Sonnier*, the jurisprudence provides a stable framework for resolving disputes while respecting both statutory law and the sacred nature of burial.

With ownership and interment rights clarified, we now turn to the next major area of litigation — **family burial grounds and the statutory meaning of "family" under Luisiana law.**

CHAPTER 7

FAMILY BURIAL GROUNDS UNDER LA. R.S. 8:1(24)

Family burial grounds occupy a special place in Louisiana law. They reflect a centuries-old tradition of burying the dead on family property, sustaining lineage across generations, and preserving the memory of ancestors on homestead land. Unlike large commercial cemeteries governed by certificates of authority and trust-fund regulations, family burial grounds operate under a different statutory structure – one that prioritizes heritage, continuity, and the rights of descendants.

This chapter explains the legal meaning of a "family burial ground," the criteria established by **La. R.S. 8:1(24)**, and the key jurisprudence that clarifies how these sites are created, inherited, regulated, and protected. The leading case in this area, *Succession of Begnaud*, serves as the most detailed judicial treatment of family burial grounds and remains essential for practitioners.

The Statutory Definition: La. R.S. 8:1(24)

A “family burial ground” is defined by **La. R.S. 8:1(24)** as:

> **§8:1. Definitions**
> (24) "Family burial ground" means a cemetery in which no lots are sold to the public and in which interments are restricted to a group of persons related to each other by blood or marriage.

Under this definition, a family burial ground is characterized by:

1. No sale of lots to the public

A statutory family burial ground must be **exclusively private.** If lots are sold to anyone outside the family, the burial ground loses its classification and may become subject to broader regulations.

2. Burial restricted to members of one family

Eligibility is limited to persons connected **by blood or marriage.** This includes adopted children through Louisiana’s civil adoption laws.

3. Recognition as an official cemetery under Title 8

Even though it is private and non-commercial, a family burial ground is still a **cemetery** in the full legal sense of Title 8.

This statutory definition forms the foundation for understanding the obligations and limitations governing family burial grounds in Louisiana.

Distinguishing Statutory Family Burial Grounds From Cemeteries "Created by Use"

Louisiana's cemetery landscape includes another important category—**family cemeteries created by use**, recognized through **jurisprudence**, not statute. This distinction is most clearly articulated in the seminal case:

Succession of Begnaud

In *Begnaud*, the court held that a burial ground may be legally recognized as a **cemetery** through **repeated use over time**, even in the absence of:

- a deed,
- a survey,
- a formal dedication, or
- recorded documentation.

This jurisprudential doctrine operates alongside the statutory definition and is essential to understand:

A "family burial ground" under La. R.S. 8:1 is a statutory category.

It requires a closed family group and no public sale of lots.

A "family cemetery created by use" is a jurisprudential category.

It may include:

- multiple generations of family burials, **and**
- burial grounds established long before formal cemetery statutes existed.

In *Begnaud*, the court held that once burials occur – whether formally dedicated or not – the land becomes encumbered with a **cemetery servitude** that persists through any change in ownership. Heirs retain permanent rights of access, and the burial ground cannot be disturbed without full compliance with state law and judicial oversight.

Why Both Concepts Matter

A family burial ground, under statute, is defined by its **rules of operation.** A family cemetery created by use is determined by **historical reality.**

For Title 8 compliance and property law, both are cemeteries – but the statutory definition governs the former. At the same time, *Begnaud* and related cases illuminate the legal consequences of the latter.

Rights of Family Members in a Statutory Family Burial Ground

Family members retain significant legal rights in a statutory family burial ground, including:

1. Right of burial within the family group

Any individual who fits the statutory relationship criteria has a right to interment, absent a contrary family rule or limitation.

2. Right of access to the cemetery

Descendants and relatives have a perpetual right to enter the burial ground to:

- visit graves,
- maintain markers,
- clean the grounds, and
- preserve the cemetery's dignity.

These rights persist **even when the underlying property changes ownership**, a principle strongly reinforced in *Begnaud.*

3. Right to preserve the cemetery

Family members may maintain fencing, gates, markers, shrubs, or other features typical of a private burial ground.

4. Right to prevent disturbance

Any proposal to relocate graves requires strict compliance with **La. R.S. 8:659** and, where unmarked or historic graves are involved, **La. R.S. 8:671–681**.

DUTIES AND LIMITATIONS ON LANDOWNERS

If a family burial ground exists on private property—whether statutory or created by use—the landowner must comply with strict legal obligations:

A landowner may <u>NOT</u>:

- deny access to descendants,
- disturb or remove remains,

- obstruct or destroy markers,
- construct improvements over graves,
- repurpose or subdivide the burial ground, or
- relocate graves without a court order.

A landowner MUST:

- maintain meaningful access,
- avoid actions that interfere with family rights,
- respect the cemetery's boundaries,
- comply with state law in any proposed changes.

These duties stem from both Title 8 and the **cemetery servitude** described in *Begnaud.*

Regulatory Oversight

The Louisiana Cemetery Board does not regulate family burial grounds in the same way as public or perpetual care cemeteries. However, they are **not exempt** from:

- Louisiana's disinterment statutes,
- state laws prohibiting desecration or disturbance of graves,
- historic and unmarked burial protections,
- parish or municipal health requirements,
- criminal penalties for interference with human remains.

Thus, while not "regulated cemeteries" in the commercial sense, they remain protected spaces in law.

Loss or Conversion of Status

A statutory family burial ground loses its classification if:

- **Lots are sold to non-family members**
- **Burials extend beyond the family group**
- **The cemetery begins serving the public**
- **It becomes part of a larger dedicated cemetery tract**

Once any of these occur, the burial ground becomes subject to a different regulatory structure under Title 8.

Conclusion

A family burial ground under **La. R.S. 8:1** is a cemetery reserved exclusively for members of a single family and is prohibited from selling lots to the public.

At the same time, Louisiana courts—most notably in *Succession of Begnaud*—recognize and protect family cemeteries created through longstanding use, even without formal dedication.

These two frameworks—statutory and jurisprudential—operate together to ensure that Louisiana's deep tradition of family burial grounds remains preserved, respected, and protected.

Understanding the distinction is essential for ensuring legal compliance, maintaining family heritage, and upholding the dignity of those interred.

CHAPTER 8

SELLING GRAVES: UNDEVELOPED LAND & MISREPRESENTATION

Among the most serious operational risks faced by Louisiana cemeteries is the sale of interment spaces on land that is not yet developed – or worse, land that the Cemetery Authority has no realistic plan or financial ability to develop. Title 8 imposes strict requirements on pre-construction sales, recognizing the potential for fraud, consumer harm, and the collapse of cemetery projects. When disputes arise, the jurisprudence treats misrepresentation in cemetery sales with exceptional seriousness.

This chapter explores the statutory framework governing the sale of undeveloped cemetery property, the landmark *Giles* case, and the obligations of Cemetery Authorities to conduct sales ethically and transparently.

THE STATUTORY FRAMEWORK: LA. R.S. 8:704 & 8:705.1

Louisiana law sharply restricts the sale of cemetery spaces on land that has not yet been prepared for burial. The governing statutes – **La. R.S. 8:704** and **La. R.S. 8:705.1** – reflect the Legislature's intent to prevent abuses that were historically common in the funeral and cemetery industry.

Under **La. R.S. 8:704**, a Cemetery Authority may not sell interment spaces in an undeveloped portion of a cemetery unless:

- the area has been duly dedicated,
- surveys or plats clearly identify the intended spaces,
- the cemetery demonstrates a plan for development, and
- representations made to purchasers are accurate and not misleading.

La. R.S. 8:705.1 further criminalizes the intentional sale of undeveloped cemetery property without compliance, creating penalties for misrepresentation and fraudulent conduct.

These statutes seek to ensure that when families purchase a burial space, they receive a legitimate, usable location – not a promise with no pathway to fulfillment.

The Problem of "Garden" or "Section" Projects

Many modern cemeteries create themed "gardens," "memorial parks," or "family estates." While perfectly lawful, these projects must be supported by realistic planning, infrastructure, and financing. Problems arise when:

- the project exists only on paper,
- development proceeds far more slowly than represented,
- the Cemetery Authority misuses funds, or
- purchasers discover years later that the promised section does not exist.

Such scenarios often give rise to litigation, with courts evaluating whether the Cemetery Authority complied with Title 8's requirements and whether purchasers were misled.

Giles v. Oak Lane Memorial Park: The Foundational Case

The leading case on undeveloped cemetery sales is *Giles v. Oak Lane Memorial Park*. In *Giles*, families purchased spaces in a new "family garden" that the cemetery had promoted as forthcoming. Years later, the area remained undeveloped, and purchasers filed suit.

The First Circuit held:

- A cemetery may not sell plots on undeveloped land without complying with **La. R.S. 8:704**.
- Misrepresentations — even unintentional ones — can justify damages, rescission, or other remedies.
- Families rely heavily on cemetery representations, and Title 8 exists to protect that reliance.
- A cemetery's failure to develop promised land constitutes a breach of statutory and contractual obligations.

The court's opinion reflects strong judicial concern about consumer protection in cemetery matters. Burial is not an ordinary transaction; it implicates dignity, familial trust, and permanent consequences.

Misrepresentation and Consumer Protection

Louisiana courts treat cemetery misrepresentation with heightened scrutiny. Because cemetery purchases involve emotional vulnerability, family grief, and long-term commitments, judges have little patience for:

- misleading maps or diagrams,
- failure to disclose development timelines,
- non-existent "premium sections,"

- inaccurate representations about trust funds,
- or unauthorized pre-construction sales.

When misrepresentation is proven, courts frequently grant:

- rescission of the contract,
- damages for emotional distress,
- refund of purchase price,
- specific performance (developing the section), or
- regulatory or criminal referrals under **La. R.S. 8:705.1**.

THE ROLE OF TRUST FUNDS AND FINANCIAL ACCOUNTABILITY

Although undeveloped-land sales fall under **La. R.S. 8:704**, the development itself often implicates cemetery trust laws. Title 8 requires:

- perpetual care deposits under **La. R.S. 8:306** and related statutes,
- proper use of merchandise-trust funds under **La. R.S. 8:605**, and
- compliance with financial oversight by the Louisiana Cemetery Board.

When cemeteries use pre-construction funds to cover unrelated expenses or cash-flow shortages, they risk violating both trust statutes and criminal provisions.

The *Giles* court highlighted this danger by scrutinizing Oak Lane's handling of purchaser funds and project financing.

Garden Projects and the "Good Faith" Standard

Cemeteries frequently ask whether they may sell burial rights in plots in a future section if they "intend" to develop the land. The jurisprudence and statutory scheme make clear:

- Good faith alone is **not sufficient.**
- The land must meet the conditions set forth in **La. R.S. 8:704**, including dedication and identifiable layout.
- Purchasers must know exactly what they are buying.
- Development must follow a realistic and documented timeline.

Cemetery Authorities cannot rely on broad aspirational plans. They must demonstrate concrete steps toward development.

Practical Guidance for Cemetery Authorities

To comply with **La. R.S. 8:704**, Cemetery Authorities should:

- Dedicate land formally before selling spaces.
- Prepare accurate plats or surveys.
- Avoid selling "future" or "conceptual" sections without infrastructure.
- Maintain transparency regarding timelines, construction, and availability.
- Place funds in required trusts and avoid diversion.
- Keep clear, permanent records of all sales, contracts, and representations.

Cemetery operators should realize that pre-construction sales are among the fastest ways to trigger a regulatory investigation or litigation.

Practical Guidance for Families, Notaries & Attorneys

Families purchasing cemetery spaces should:

- request maps, plats, or physical tours of the actual section,
- confirm the land has been developed or dedicated,
- request written timelines for development,
- ensure all contracts comply with **La. R.S. 8:704**,
- and verify that funds are placed in the appropriate trusts.

Notaries preparing cemetery purchase agreements should include:

- disclosure language about development status,
- acknowledgment of plats and maps,
- statements of compliance with Title 8, and
- signatures from authorized cemetery representatives.

Attorneys should investigate claims of "phantom gardens," delayed development, and failure to deposit trust funds as potential violations of **La. R.S. 8:704** and **La. R.S. 8:705.1**.

Conclusion

The sale of undeveloped cemetery property is one of the most tightly regulated areas of Louisiana cemetery law. Through **La. R.S. 8:704**, **La. R.S. 8:705.1**, and the judicial guidance provided by *Giles*, the law protects families from misleading sales practices and ensures that burial locations offered for purchase are real, identifiable, and properly developed.

These protections underscore the Legislature's commitment to dignity, consumer fairness, and transparency in cemetery operations – values essential to maintaining trust in an industry that deals with life's most sensitive moments.

With consumer protection addressed, the next chapter turns to another major area of litigation: **perpetual care, merchandise trusts, and the limits of the Louisiana Cemetery Board's authority.**

CHAPTER 9

PERPETUAL CARE: THE LIMITS OF REGULATORY AUTHORITY

Perpetual care is the financial backbone of modern cemetery operations. The concept is simple: a portion of every burial-space sale (at least 10%) must be placed into a trust fund, which generates income for the ongoing maintenance of the cemetery grounds. But the legal structure behind perpetual care is anything but simple. Louisiana's trust-fund statutes, found throughout Title 8, impose strict duties on Cemetery Authorities, trustees, and regulators – and disputes over these funds frequently rise to the level of appellate litigation.

The most significant case in this arena, *Westlawn Cemeteries, L.L.C. v. Louisiana Cemetery Board*, reshaped the relationship between cemetery operators and the Louisiana Cemetery Board (LCB), placing constitutional limits on the Board's regulatory powers. This chapter explores the statutory framework, the Westlawn decision, and the broader implications for cemetery governance.

The Statutory Framework of Title 8 Trust Requirements

Louisiana's cemetery trust laws are scattered across several key sections:

- **La. R.S. 8:301–8:306** govern perpetual care cemeteries.
- **La. R.S. 8:306** in particular requires deposits into a perpetual care fund.
- **La. R.S. 8:605** and related statutes govern merchandise-trust funds.
- **La. R.S. 8:406** and related sections address religious-cemetery exceptions.
- **La. R.S. 8:304** imposes certificate-of-authority requirements (with trust implications for for-profit cemeteries).

These statutes collectively mandate that:

- a portion of every sale be deposited in trust,
- the trust be irrevocable,
- funds be used only for maintenance and care,
- trustees submit annual reports,
- and cemeteries maintain compliance subject to LCB oversight.

The Legislature intended these funds to guarantee that cemeteries remain maintained far into the future, even if ownership changes or burial sales decline.

The Role of the Louisiana Cemetery Board (LCB)

The LCB is empowered to:

- audit cemetery perpetual care and merchandise-trust funds,
- require annual financial reports,
- issue or revoke certificates of authority,
- promulgate rules under the Administrative Procedure Act, and
- enforce compliance through administrative actions and fines.

However, the Board's authority is not unlimited. Title 8 restricts the LCB to powers explicitly granted by statute, and the Louisiana Constitution prohibits agencies from expanding their authority through rulemaking beyond what the Legislature has authorized.

This constitutional limit became the central issue in *Westlawn.*

WESTLAWN CEMETERIES, L.L.C. V. LOUISIANA CEMETERY BOARD

In *Westlawn,* the Louisiana Cemetery Board adopted a rule – formerly **LAC 46:XIII.1503(C)** – requiring additional perpetual care trust deposits beyond those specified in Title 8. Westlawn challenged the rule, arguing that:

- The Board exceeded its statutory authority;
- The rule conflicted with the Legislature's specific deposit requirements;
- The Board had, in effect, created a new financial obligation not provided for by law.

The case reached the Louisiana Supreme Court, which agreed with Westlawn.

The Court held:

1. **Administrative agencies may not expand statutory obligations through rulemaking.**
2. The LCB's perpetual care rule imposed requirements **not authorized** by **La. R.S. 8:301–8:306.**
3. The rule violated the **separation of powers** by encroaching on the Legislature's domain.
4. Because the rule was unconstitutional as applied, Westlawn was entitled to relief.

This decision fundamentally reshaped how the Board exercises its regulatory authority and reaffirmed that Title 8 trust requirements are governed by statute — not administrative creativity.

Implications for Cemetery Authorities

The *Westlawn* decision clarified and reinforced several principles that directly affect cemetery operators:

- **Trust deposit requirements come only from statute**, not from LCB rules.
- The Board may require compliance, reporting, and audits — but may not invent new financial obligations.
- Cemeteries must still keep meticulous trust records and demonstrate compliance with **La. R.S. 8:306** and related statutes.
- Violations of Title 8 may still lead to enforcement actions, but such actions must be grounded in the statutes themselves.

For Cemetery Authorities, *Westlawn* was both liberating and cautionary: liberating in limiting overregulation, but cautionary in emphasizing the non-negotiable nature of statutory compliance.

Merchandise Trusts and Statutory Compliance

While *Westlawn* addressed perpetual care, merchandise-trust violations under **La. R.S. 8:605** remain a common source of litigation and regulatory action. Issues often arise when cemeteries:

- use merchandise-trust funds for general operating expenses,
- fail to deposit the required amounts on time,
- or commingle trust funds with other accounts.

Violations can lead to:

- restitution orders,
- administrative penalties,
- suspension of certificates of authority (under **La. R.S. 8:304**),
- and in egregious cases, criminal exposure.

The LCB regularly audits merchandise-trust compliance, and courts view misuse of these funds as a serious breach of fiduciary and statutory duty.

Trustees' Responsibilities

Trustees – often banks or financial institutions – hold significant responsibilities under Title 8. They must:

- safeguard trust assets,
- ensure proper investment under Louisiana trust law,
- provide annual reports to Cemetery Authorities and the LCB,
- and refuse improper withdrawal requests.

If trustees fail to meet these obligations, litigation may be brought against them directly. Trust mismanagement cases frequently involve dual claims: one against the Cemetery Authority for improper depositing, and one against the trustee for improper administration.

Transparency, Recordkeeping, and Public Confidence

The Legislature designed Title 8's trust structure to promote transparency. Courts and regulators consistently highlight the importance of:

- accurate trust ledgers,
- timely reporting under **La. R.S. 8:306**,
- records of deposits tied to specific contracts,

- clearly segregated accounts,
- and consumer access to certain financial assurances.

When trust records are incomplete, courts often infer mismanagement or bad faith – creating significant exposure for cemeteries.

Practical Guidance for Cemetery Authorities

To comply with Title 8 and avoid litigation:

- Deposit trust funds at the moment of sale or within the statutory timeframe.
- Maintain separate perpetual care and merchandise-trust accounts.
- Document every deposit and withdrawal.
- Review trust reports annually with professional advisors.
- Ensure all rules governing trust withdrawals are followed meticulously.
- Respond promptly to LCB audit requests.
- Maintain internal policies aligned with statutory – not administrative – requirements.

Cemeteries should treat trust compliance as a core operational obligation, not a mere regulatory formality.

PRACTICAL GUIDANCE FOR FAMILIES, NOTARIES & ATTORNEYS

For consumers and professionals:

- Ask whether perpetual care and merchandise funds are compliant with **La. R.S. 8:306** and **La. R.S. 8:605.**
- Request contract copies showing required deposit amounts.
- Evaluate whether cemetery representations match statutory requirements.
- In litigation, examine trust ledgers early – they often reveal the core problem.

Attorneys representing families or purchasers should scrutinize trust-related claims in cases involving undeveloped land, delayed delivery of merchandise, or general mismanagement of a cemetery.

CONCLUSION

Trust funds are the financial foundation of cemetery care in Louisiana. Through Title 8 and Westlawn's guidance, the law establishes a careful balance: Cemetery Authorities must faithfully maintain perpetual care and merchandise trusts, and regulators must enforce statutory obligations without exceeding their authority.

The *Westlawn* decision protects both consumers and cemetery operators by clarifying that only the Legislature sets the financial rules – a vital boundary in an industry built on trust, permanence, and dignity.

With the financial structure of cemetery operations addressed, the next chapter turns to a very different field: **public law, expropriation, and the status of abandoned or historic cemeteries in Louisiana**

PRACTICE GUIDANCE FOR FAMILIES, NOTARIES & ATTORNEYS

[illegible]

[illegible]

[illegible]

CONCLUSION

[illegible]

[illegible]

[illegible] in Louisiana

CHAPTER 10

ABANDONMENT & THE FATE OF HISTORIC CEMETERIES

Cemeteries are among the most protected spaces in Louisiana law. Yet, history shows that development, infrastructure projects, urban expansion, and neglect sometimes threaten cemeteries. When public entities seek to expropriate cemetery property – or when cemeteries fall into disuse – courts must balance the dignity of the dead with the practical needs of the living. Louisiana's jurisprudence demonstrates an unwavering commitment to the principle that burial places deserve special legal protection and may be disturbed only under the most compelling circumstances.

This chapter examines the landmark cases that define the limits of expropriation and abandonment, the statutory framework governing cemetery relocation, and the distinctions between historic cemeteries and neglected burial sites.

The Foundational Principle: Cemeteries Are Not Ordinary Property

Louisiana courts have consistently held that cemeteries occupy a unique legal status that elevates them beyond the standard rules of immovable property. They are:

- places of reverence,
- repositories of human remains,
- protected cultural sites, and
- subject to heightened judicial scrutiny.

This principle is anchored in two landmark Louisiana Supreme Court decisions:

- *City of New Orleans v. Christ Church Corp.* (1955), and
- *Touro Synagogue v. Goodwill Industries* (1957).

These cases set the doctrinal foundation for how cemetery land is treated when public authorities attempt to expropriate or modify burial sites.

City of New Orleans v. Christ Church: Expropriation Limits

In *Christ Church,* the City of New Orleans sought to expropriate the historic Girod Street Cemetery for urban development. The cemetery had fallen into severe neglect, and the City argued that removal was necessary for public welfare.

The Louisiana Supreme Court disagreed, holding:

- Cemetery land cannot be expropriated like ordinary immovable property.
- Burial grounds are protected by public policy and religious liberty principles.
- Even when a cemetery is in poor condition, its status as a burial place imposes restrictions on governmental action.
- Expropriation is permissible only when **explicit statutory authority** exists and when the public purpose is sufficiently compelling.

The Court insisted that the remains be handled respectfully and under judicial supervision, setting a precedent for all future cemetery removal efforts.

TOURO SYNAGOGUE V. GOODWILL INDUSTRIES: REINFORCING PROTECTION

Two years later, in *Touro Synagogue*, the Court again confronted questions about the transfer of cemetery property. The issue involved ownership rights in a Jewish cemetery and whether the land could be alienated.

The Court reaffirmed the core principles from *Christ Church*:

- Burial grounds cannot be freely sold or repurposed without statutory authority.
- Religious, cultural, and historical dimensions strengthen protections surrounding cemeteries.
- Property law yields to the public interest in preserving burial sites.

Touro makes clear that even when ownership of cemetery land transfers, the cemetery's status as a burial ground persists unless and until legally extinguished.

ABANDONMENT OF CEMETERIES: LEGAL MYTHS AND REALITIES

Many assume that a cemetery becomes "abandoned" when families no longer visit, when burials cease, or when maintenance lapses. Louisiana law rejects this assumption.

A cemetery is **not** abandoned simply because:

- it is overgrown,
- the ownership is unclear,
- no burials have occurred in decades, or
- No one actively maintains the grounds.

Instead, abandonment has a legal meaning tied to statutory procedures – particularly under:

- the cemetery relocation statutes **(La. R.S. 8:659)**,
- municipal powers for neglected property,
- and the Unmarked Human Burial Sites Preservation Act **(La. R.S. 8:671–681)**.

Even "abandoned" cemeteries remain cemeteries until the remains are lawfully relocated.

HISTORIC CEMETERIES AND PUBLIC POLICY

In Louisiana, historic cemeteries enjoy special protection because they reflect the state's diverse cultural heritage – Acadian, Creole, Indigenous, African, Jewish, Catholic, and Protestant traditions. Courts and regulators treat historic cemeteries with heightened sensitivity.

Under the Historic Cemetery Preservation Act **(La. R.S. 25:931–943)**:

- Historic cemeteries may not be altered, demolished, or relocated without compliance with preservation requirements.
- The State Historic Preservation Officer (SHPO) plays an oversight role.
- Violations may result in civil penalties and restoration orders.

These statutes underscore that many cemetery disputes are not merely private matters but issues of cultural preservation.

The Role of La. R.S. 8:659 in Cemetery Removal

While earlier chapters focused on **La. R.S. 8:659**, which governs disinterment among families, also regulates the mass removal of remains from cemeteries threatened by development or public projects.

The statute requires:

- consent of the Cemetery Authority,
- consent of the statutory decision-makers, or
- if consent cannot be obtained, a **court order**.

Courts applying **La. R.S. 8:659** in removal cases insist on:

- notice to descendants when identifiable,
- careful documentation,
- respectful handling of remains, and
- compliance with public health and archaeological standards.

Even when the State or a municipality seeks removal, judicial oversight is mandatory.

Unmarked and Lost Cemeteries: La. R.S. 8:671–681

The Unmarked Human Burial Sites Preservation Act (**La. R.S. 8:671–681**) protects ancient, forgotten, or accidental burial sites, including Native American and archaeological burials.

When human remains are discovered:

- Work must cease immediately.
- The Division of Archaeology must be notified.
- Removal may occur only after consultation with tribal authorities, descendants, or cultural representatives.
- Violations may incur penalties, including seizure of artifacts and civil liability.

This statutory scheme reflects profound respect for Louisiana's layered history and ensures that unmarked sites receive the same dignity as formal cemeteries.

PUBLIC VS. PRIVATE INTERESTS

Whenever the fate of a cemetery is at stake, Louisiana courts weigh competing interests:

Public Interests

- infrastructure development (roads, levees, drainage)
- public safety
- environmental health
- blight remediation

Private Interests

- property rights of the landowner
- burial rights of families
- cultural and religious interests of communities

Courts consistently prioritize **dignity, preservation, and statutory compliance**, but also recognize that public welfare may justify relocation when conducted lawfully and respectfully.

PRACTICAL GUIDANCE FOR MUNICIPALITIES, DEVELOPERS & LANDOWNERS

When dealing with property that may contain cemeteries:

- Conduct surveys and historical research early.
- Do not disturb suspected burial grounds without consulting the appropriate authorities.
- Seek legal guidance on **La. R.S. 8:659**, **La. R.S. 8:671–681**, and **La. R.S. 25:931–943**.
- In development projects, coordinate with archaeologists and SHPO.
- Secure judicial authorization before removing remains.
- Document all movement of remains carefully.

Ignoring these requirements exposes parties to severe legal, financial, and reputational consequences.

PRACTICAL GUIDANCE FOR FAMILIES & DESCENDANTS

Families who learn that a cemetery is threatened should:

- request notice and documentation,
- contact SHPO or the Division of Archaeology when appropriate,
- consult with legal counsel regarding **La. R.S. 8:659**, and
- consider seeking injunctive relief to halt unlawful disturbance.

Courts frequently side with families when cemetery removal attempts do not comply with statutory protections.

CONCLUSION

Cemeteries – whether historic, active, neglected, or tucked away on private land – are not ordinary real estate. Louisiana's courts and statutes treat them as sacred spaces whose disturbance requires compelling reasons and strict compliance with legal procedures. Through *Christ Church*, *Touro Synagogue*, and the detailed statutory framework of Title 8 and the Historic Cemetery Preservation Act, Louisiana law ensures that the fate of burial places is never determined lightly.

With expropriation and historic preservation addressed, the next chapter turns to another sensitive dimension of cemetery jurisprudence: **unmarked burial sites, archaeological protections, and the duties of the State when the dead are found beyond traditional cemeteries.**

CHAPTER II

UNMARKED BURIAL SITES & ARCHAEOLOGICAL PROTECTIONS

Not all burial places in Louisiana are formal cemeteries. Many are older than the state itself: Indigenous burial mounds, colonial graveyards, plantation burials, enslaved-person cemeteries, rural homestead plots, and forgotten nineteenth-century epidemics sites. These locations often lack headstones, boundaries, or records. Yet, when human remains are encountered, Louisiana law treats them with the same dignity and seriousness as any modern cemetery.

This chapter explains the legal framework that protects unmarked burial sites, the role of the Division of Archaeology, the procedural requirements for discovery, and the practical responsibilities of landowners, professionals, and public authorities. The guiding statutes – **La. R.S. 8:671–681** (Unmarked Human Burial Sites Preservation Act) and **La. R.S. 25:931–943** (Historic Cemetery Preservation Act) – form one of the strongest burial-protection regimes in the country.

The Unmarked Human Burial Sites Preservation Act: La. R.S. 8:671–681

The Unmarked Human Burial Sites Preservation Act (**La. R.S. 8:671–681**) was enacted to protect ancient or forgotten burial locations that surface through excavation, natural erosion, infrastructure projects, or agricultural work.

The Act applies to:

- prehistoric burials,
- Indigenous burial mounds,
- colonial or antebellum burials,
- unrecorded family plots,
- suspected slave cemeteries,
- informal burial grounds without visible markers.

Its purpose is preservation, investigation, and respectful treatment — not destruction or relocation for convenience.

Immediate Duties Upon Discovery of Human Remains

When human remains or burial objects are encountered, **Louisiana law imposes immediate and non-negotiable obligations**:

1. **Work must stop immediately.**
2. The discoverer must notify local law enforcement.
3. Law enforcement will determine whether the remains are part of a crime scene.
4. If the remains are not part of an active criminal investigation, law enforcement must notify the **Division of Archaeology.**

5. The Division becomes the lead agency for determining the nature of the burial, archaeological significance, and the proper next steps.

Failure to stop work may result in civil penalties and criminal liability under **La. R.S. 8:679** and related provisions.

ROLE OF THE DIVISION OF ARCHAEOLOGY

The Division of Archaeology (part of the Louisiana Office of Cultural Development) has broad responsibilities under **La. R.S. 8:671–681**, including:

- conducting field assessments,
- determining whether the site is an unmarked cemetery,
- identifying cultural or tribal affiliation,
- consulting with descendant communities,
- developing a treatment plan for preservation or relocation,
- coordinating with federal authorities when applicable (e.g., NAGPRA).

For Indigenous burials, consultation with tribal governments is mandatory. The Division plays both a scientific and a cultural role, ensuring that burial sites are not treated as mere artifacts, but as sacred resting places.

Removal & Relocation of Unmarked Remains

The Act strongly favors preservation. Removal is permitted only under limited circumstances and requires:

- approval from the Division of Archaeology,
- a written treatment plan,
- attempts to identify descendants or cultural stakeholders,
- and compliance with **La. R.S. 8:659** if relocation is sought.

The statutory interplay is important: while **La. R.S. 8:659** governs disinterment in recognized cemeteries, the Unmarked Burial Sites Act controls when burials are unknown, ancient, or archaeologically significant.

Courts require meticulous documentation before approving relocation.

Penalties for Disturbance

Violating the Unmarked Human Burial Sites Preservation Act carries significant consequences. Under **La. R.S. 8:679**, penalties may include:

- civil fines,
- restitution for damage,
- seizure of artifacts,
- court orders requiring restoration or mitigation.

Knowingly disturbing an unmarked burial site is treated as a serious offense reflecting Louisiana's deep cultural respect for the dead.

HISTORIC CEMETERY PRESERVATION ACT: LA. R.S. 25:931–943

While **La. R.S. 8:671–681** focuses on unmarked burials, the Historic Cemetery Preservation Act **(La. R.S. 25:931–943)** protects older cemeteries of documented historical value.

A historic cemetery may be:

- publicly recognized on state or federal registers, or
- simply determined to be of cultural significance by the State Historic Preservation Officer (SHPO).

The Act prohibits:

- demolition,
- alteration,
- desecration, or
- removal

without compliance with its procedures and approvals.

Civil penalties and injunctive relief are available to prevent unlawful destruction.

THE INTERSECTION OF ARCHAEOLOGY, CULTURE & LAW

Unmarked burial sites often connect with broader cultural narratives – Indigenous history, African diaspora history, immigration, epidemics, or forgotten parish communities. Courts and regulators, therefore, approach these cases with cultural sensitivity.

When determining the treatment of unmarked remains, the Division of Archaeology may consult:

- tribal governments,
- descendant families,
- religious leaders,
- cultural historians,
- municipal authorities.

This interdisciplinary model reflects Louisiana's recognition that burial sites are not simply legal obstacles but essential elements of cultural heritage.

Landowner Responsibilities

Landowners who discover remains on their property must adhere strictly to:

- **La. R.S. 8:671–681**,
- **La. R.S. 25:931–943**,
- and where applicable, **La. R.S. 8:659**.

Best practices include:

- halting all earth work,
- securing the site,
- contacting law enforcement and the Division of Archaeology,
- cooperating with investigators,
- avoiding media exposure until facts are known,
- retaining legal counsel when necessary.

Landowners are not financially responsible for archaeological assessments unless they seek to relocate the cemetery for development. However, they must not interfere with preservation efforts.

Responsibilities of Municipalities, Developers & Contractors

Cities, developers, utilities, and contractors must incorporate burial-site risk assessments into project planning early. This includes:

- historical research,
- ground-penetrating radar (GPR) surveys,
- permitting compliance,
- written protocols for accidental discovery,
- training field personnel on reporting obligations.

Large infrastructure projects — drainage, road expansion, levee work, industrial sites — frequently encounter unmarked burials, and noncompliance can halt projects indefinitely.

Practical Guidance for Clergy & Families

Clergy may be involved when unmarked remains are identified as belonging to faith communities. Their roles include:

- advising descendants,
- participating in reburial ceremonies,
- helping document genealogical context,
- assisting cultural or religious consultations.

Families should be aware that they have rights in these situations, even when the burial location was previously unknown. The law seeks to restore dignity to forgotten remains, not to erase them.

Conclusion

Unmarked burial sites reveal the hidden history of Louisiana – often painful, always important. Through **La. R.S. 8:671–681** and **La. R.S. 25:931–943**, the State ensures that accidental discoveries become moments of reverence rather than destruction. These statutes, supported by archaeology and jurisprudence, protect both the dignity of the dead and the cultural memory of the living.

With unmarked and historic burials addressed, the next chapter turns to **the practical, day-to-day application of cemetery case law in real cemetery administration.**

CHAPTER 12

USING CASE LAW IN EVERYDAY CEMETERY ADMINISTRATION

The preceding chapters analyze Louisiana's major cemetery cases and statutes in detail. But jurisprudence is not merely academic – it is a practical tool for Cemetery Authorities, notaries, clergy, attorneys, and municipal officials who navigate burial decisions every day. This chapter synthesizes the lessons of the case law and shows how Louisiana cemeteries can use these principles to create clear, lawful, and pastoral administrative policies.

Case law offers a road map. When administrators understand how courts interpret **La. R.S. 8:655, La. R.S. 8:659, La. R.S. 8:660, La. R.S. 8:704, La. R.S. 8:705.1**, and other statutes, they gain the ability to prevent disputes, respond lawfully to difficult situations, and protect their cemetery from litigation.

The Core Insight: Documentation Controls Everything

In every cemetery case – *Sonnier, Spiess, Pittman, Gilmore, Giles, Begnaud, Westlawn* – the presence or absence of documentation determines the outcome. The courts repeatedly emphasize that written records, not memories or verbal statements, carry legal weight.

Cemetery Authorities should therefore maintain:

- written declarations of interment authority under **La. R.S. 8:655**,
- written consent for disinterment under **La. R.S. 8:659**,
- contracts, deeds, maps, plats, and transfer records under **La. R.S. 8:802–804**,
- trust-fund documentation required by **La. R.S. 8:301–8:306** and **La. R.S. 8:605**,
- records of ownership disputes or family communications,
- photo documentation of tombs, lot numbers, and burial locations.

A cemetery with strong documentation wins disputes before they begin.

Applying the Sonnier Rule: Identifying the Correct Decision-Maker

Every burial and disinterment must be authorized by the correct person in the **La. R.S. 8:655** hierarchy. To avoid litigation:

- Do not rely on verbal statements from family members.
- Verify identity and priority using the statutory list.
- Require signatures from all persons in the same class (e.g., adult children or parents).
- Request marriage certificates or successions documents when necessary.
- Reject military PADDs for civilian burials unless supported by Louisiana law.

Checklist for Burial Authorization

- ✓ Did the decedent leave a notarized declaration?
- ✓ If not, who is the highest-ranked living person under the statute?
- ✓ Are there multiple people in that class? If so, all must consent.
- ✓ Are there blended-family issues, estranged relatives, or minors involved?
- ✓ Is documentation sufficient to protect the cemetery from liability?

Using this checklist aligns daily operations with *Sonnier* and prevents the disputes that filled the appellate record in that case.

Applying the Spiess–Pittman Rule: Handling Disinterment Requests

Under **La. R.S. 8:659**, disinterment requires strict legal compliance. Case law teaches:

- Treat disinterment as an extraordinary event.
- Obtain signatures from all required persons under **La. R.S. 8:659**.
- Do not rely on burial rights ownership alone (per *Sonnier*).
- Refer disputed cases to court.
- Maintain a written disinterment policy consistent with **La. R.S. 8:660**.

Disinterment Steps for Cemetery Authorities

1. Receive written request.
2. Identify statutory decision-makers under **La. R.S. 8:655**.
3. Inform all necessary parties.
4. Obtain written consent from all persons in the same class.
5. Require a court order if any objection exists.
6. Coordinate safe removal under **La. R.S. 8:660**.
7. Document every step.

These steps reflect the reasoning in *Spiess* and *Pittman*, ensuring compliance and reducing emotional conflict.

Applying the Giles Rule: Sales of Undeveloped Land

The *Giles* decision provides essential guidance for avoiding consumer-protection violations:

- Never sell burial spaces on undeveloped land without full compliance with **La. R.S. 8:704**.
- Avoid conceptual maps or "coming soon" gardens unless development is imminent and documented.
- Disclose development timelines in writing.
- Do not use pre-construction payments as operating funds.
- Maintain trust deposits under **La. R.S. 8:306** and **La. R.S. 8:605**.

Cemetery Authorities should incorporate *Giles*-compliant language into all sales contracts, brochures, and marketing materials.

Applying the Westlawn Rule: Understanding Regulatory Limits

The *Westlawn* case reshaped the relationship between cemeteries and the Louisiana Cemetery Board:

- The LCB cannot impose trust-fund obligations not expressly found in Title 8.
- Cemeteries must comply with **La. R.S. 8:301–8:306**, but not with unconstitutional rules.
- Audits and reporting remain mandatory, but financial rulemaking is limited.

Cemetery operators should:

- Review trust practices annually,
- Work closely with trustees,
- Respond to LCB audits promptly,
- Ensure compliance with statutes, not assumptions.

Applying Begnaud: Understanding Family Burial Grounds

When operating or advising on family cemeteries under **La. R.S. 8:1(24)**:

- Remember that family burial grounds arise by use, not by deed.
- Heirs have access rights even if ownership passes to unrelated persons.
- Burial eligibility is guided by family tradition and statutory recognition.
- Relocation requires compliance with **La. R.S. 8:659**.

Administrators should be cautious when advising families about using family burial land for new development or sales.

Risk-Reduction Tools for Cemetery Authorities

To operationalize case law, every cemetery should adopt:

1. **A Written Burial Authorization Policy**
   - Citing *Sonnier* and **La. R.S. 8:655**.
2. **A Written Disinterment Policy**
   - Citing *Spiess*, *Pittman*, and **La. R.S. 8:659–660**.
3. **Sales & Marketing Compliance Standards**
   - Based on *Giles*, **La. R.S. 8:704**, and **La. R.S. 8:705.1**.
4. **A Trust-Fund Compliance Manual**
   - Reflecting *Westlawn* and **La. R.S. 8:301–8:306**.
5. **An Ownership-Transfer Procedure**
   - Consistent with **La. R.S. 8:802–804**.
6. **A Recordkeeping Protocol**
   - Aligning with Chapter 9 of the LCB regulations and supports litigation defense.
7. **A Family-Burial-Ground Advisory Guide**
   - Based on *Begnaud* and **La. R.S. 8:1(24)**.

These tools convert jurisprudence into operational confidence.

Clergy, Funeral Directors, & Notaries Use Case Law

Clergy

- Confirm authority to conduct a burial under **La. R.S. 8:655**.
- Facilitate family consensus in complex situations.
- Document burial locations for parish or church archives.

Funeral Directors

- Verify right-of-disposition documentation.
- Avoid relying solely on family representations.
- Coordinate with Cemetery Authorities to ensure statutory compliance.

Notaries

- Draft declarations under **La. R.S. 8:655**.
- Authenticate interment-right transfers under **La. R.S. 8:802–804**.
- Advice on family burial grounds and successions.

Each professional plays a vital role in preventing disputes before they ever reach a courthouse.

Conclusion

Cemetery jurisprudence is not merely a set of appellate opinions – it is a practical guide for daily administration. When Cemetery Authorities and allied professionals rely on case law to inform their policies and practices, they strengthen operational integrity, reduce conflict, and protect the dignity of the deceased.

With this practical foundation established, the final chapter will explore **sample forms, clauses, and litigation checklists** derived directly from Louisiana's cemetery case law.

CHAPTER 13

FORMS, CLAUSES & LITIGATION CHECKLISTS INFORMED BY CASE LAW

The value of Louisiana cemetery jurisprudence lies not only in legal interpretation but in its practical application. Courts tell us what went wrong in past disputes – and these lessons can be used to craft forms, contracts, and procedures that prevent future litigation. This chapter provides model clauses, recommended form language, and litigation checklists directly derived from *Sonnier*, *Spiess*, *Pittman*, *Gilmore*, *Begnaud*, *Giles*, *Westlawn*, and the statutory framework of Title 8.

These materials are designed for Cemetery Authorities, attorneys, notaries, and clergy who must document burial-related decisions with precision and pastoral sensitivity.

Model Clauses for Burial Authorization (La. R.S. 8:655)

1. Right of Disposition Verification Clause

To be included in all burial contracts and authorization forms:

*"Pursuant to **La. R.S. 8:655**, I certify that I am the highest-ranking person in the statutory order of priority authorized to control the disposition of the remains of the decedent. I further certify that no other person in the same class has objected to this disposition, and that all signatures of persons in the same class are attached hereto."*

This clause is derived from *Sonnier* and prevents unilateral decisions by equal-ranked family members.

2. Multi–Decision-Maker Consent Clause

For situations involving multiple children, parents, or siblings:

*"All persons in the statutory class identified under **La. R.S. 8:655** have been notified and have provided written consent for this burial. A complete list of consenting persons is attached."*

This protects cemeteries from disputes like *Sobolak*.

3. Documentation & Identification Clause

"Cemetery Authority has verified identity and priority using government-issued identification, succession documents (if applicable), and supporting records. All documentation shall be retained as part of the cemetery's permanent records in accordance with Chapter 9 of the LCB regulations."

Recordkeeping failures appear in nearly every case — this clause codifies compliance.

MODEL CLAUSES FOR DISINTERMENT (LA. R.S. 8:659–660)

1. Consent Verification Clause

*"In accordance with **La. R.S. 8:659,** written consent for disinterment has been obtained from all persons exercising the right of disposition under **La. R.S. 8:655,** and from the Cemetery Authority. No person with higher or equal priority has objected."*

2. Disputed-Consent Clause

*"If any required person refuses consent or cannot be located after reasonable effort, the Cemetery Authority shall require a court order pursuant to **La. R.S. 8:659(C)** before proceeding."*

This clause reflects the rule in *Spiess* and *Pittman* that trial courts have broad discretion, and cemeteries should not act without judicial authorization.

3. Operational Conditions Clause

*"All disinterment activities shall be performed in accordance with the cemetery's disinterment policy as authorized by **La. R.S. 8:660,** including safety, scheduling, equipment, personnel, and protective measures."*

This ensures Cemetery Authority retains operational control, consistent with Title 8.

Model Clauses for Sales of Interment Rights (La. R.S. 8:802–804)

1. Transfer Recording Clause

"Any transfer of interment rights shall be recorded in the cemetery's ownership records as required by ***La. R.S. 8:802–804****, and shall not be effective until acknowledged and approved by the Cemetery Authority."*

2. Ownership vs. Interment Rights Clarification Clause

"Owning burial rights in a cemetery space does not confer authority to determine who may be interred therein. Burial authority is governed exclusively by ***La. R.S. 8:655.****"*

This clause addresses confusion evident in the *Sonnier* litigation.

Model Clauses for Undeveloped Land Sales (La. R.S. 8:704 & 8:705.1)

1. Development Status Disclosure

"The interment space described herein is located in a section that is [developed / under development / not yet developed]. Sales in undeveloped sections are governed by ***La. R.S. 8:704****, and the cemetery acknowledges compliance with all statutory requirements."*

2. Anti-Misrepresentation Clause

"No representation regarding section completion, landscaping, structures, or features beyond those included in official plats or filings shall be construed as binding. All promotional materials must comply with ***La. R.S. 8:705.1.****"*

This language helps prevent *Giles*-type disputes.

Model Clauses for Perpetual Care & Merchandise Trusts

1. Trust Deposit Certification

"Perpetual care deposits required under ***La. R.S. 8:301–8:306*** *and merchandise-trust deposits required under* ***La. R.S. 8:605*** *shall be made within the statutory period. Documentation of deposits shall be maintained as permanent records."*

2. Regulatory Compliance Clause

"Nothing in this agreement shall be construed to impose trust-fund obligations not authorized by Title 8. The parties recognize the constitutional limits on administrative rulemaking affirmed in Westlawn Cemeteries, L.L.C. v. Louisiana Cemetery Board."

This clause protects against unconstitutional or non-statutory demands.

LITIGATION CHECKLISTS

These checklists provide a fast, defensible process when disputes arise.

Checklist A: Burial Dispute (La. R.S. 8:655)

- ✓ Identify the highest-priority person under the statute.
- ✓ Verify with ID, marriage certificate, and succession documents.
- ✓ Obtain signatures of all required persons in the same class.
- ✓ Document any dissent.
- ✓ Pause burial if a dispute exists – request a court order.
- ✓ Preserve all communications.

Checklist B: Disinterment Dispute (La. R.S. 8:659–660)

- ✓ Obtain a written request for disinterment.
- ✓ Identify all statutory decision-makers.
- ✓ Obtain unanimous consent within the class.
- ✓ If there is dissent, require a court order.
- ✓ Document operational plan under **La. R.S. 8:660**.
- ✓ Maintain chain-of-custody for remains.
- ✓ File and preserve all documentation permanently.

CHECKLIST C: UNDEVELOPED-LAND DISPUTES (LA. R.S. 8:704 & 8:705.1)

- ✓ Confirm whether the section was developed at the time of sale.
- ✓ Review plats, dedication documents, and maps.
- ✓ Check compliance with statutory requirements.
- ✓ Investigate trust deposits and merchandise delivery.
- ✓ Assess misrepresentations or omissions.
- ✓ Analyze damages and consumer-protection claims.

CHECKLIST D: TRUST-FUND LITIGATION (PERPETUAL CARE & MERCHANDISE)

- ✓ Secure all trust ledgers and bank records.
- ✓ Verify statutory deposits under **La. R.S. 8:306** and **La. R.S. 8:605.**
- ✓ Assess compliance with reporting requirements.
- ✓ Identify rulemaking issues in light of *Westlawn.*
- ✓ Evaluate trustee conduct for fiduciary breaches.
- ✓ Determine restitution or regulatory remedies.

CHECKLIST E: FAMILY BURIAL GROUND DISPUTES (LA. R.S. 8:1(24))

- ✓ Determine whether multiple family burials exist.
- ✓ Identify heirs and lineage.
- ✓ Assess access rights across private land.
- ✓ Review any attempts at removal under **La. R.S. 8:659**.
- ✓ Document historical or customary burial practices.
- ✓ Evaluate whether preservation laws apply.
- ✓ Determine restitution or regulatory remedies.

CONCLUSION

Cemetery case law provides a rich foundation for creating robust forms, policies, and contracts that protect both families and Cemetery Authorities. When administrators incorporate the principles from Louisiana's key cases into their daily practices, they reduce conflict, enhance transparency, and ensure compliance with Title 8.

With these forms and checklists established, the final chapter will look ahead – identifying trends, legislative gaps, and future directions in Louisiana cemetery law.

CHAPTER 14

FUTURE DIRECTIONS & LEGISLATIVE RECOMMENDATIONS

Cemetery law in Louisiana continues to evolve. While Title 8 provides a comprehensive framework for burial, interment rights, disinterment, perpetual care, undeveloped land, and family cemeteries, the jurisprudence reveals gaps, ambiguities, and modern challenges that the Legislature may eventually need to address. As families become more diverse, burial trends shift, and historic preservation concerns intensify, Louisiana will face new pressures that test the limits of current law.

This chapter identifies emerging issues, highlights areas where courts have struggled for clarity, and proposes legislative refinements that could strengthen cemetery governance and reduce litigation.

Emerging Trends in Louisiana Cemetery Law

1. The Rise of Blended & Non-Traditional Families

Louisiana's right of disposition statute – **La. R.S. 8:655** – assumes traditional family structures. Courts have seen increasing disputes involving:

- stepchildren and stepparents,
- unmarried partners,
- adopted and estranged children,
- second spouses competing with adult children,
- families fractured by long-standing conflict.

Cases like *Sonnier* and *Sobolak* show how courts struggle to apply rigid hierarchies to complex modern relationships. Legislative reform may be needed to:

- clarify equal-priority classes,
- define "surviving spouse" in contested circumstances,
- expand recognition of designated agents or partners,
- or streamline burdensome multi-signature requirements.

2. The Growth of Cremation

Cremation rates continue to rise, yet Title 8 is still written primarily for traditional ground burials. Questions that increasingly arise include:

- who controls the disposition of cremated remains,
- what constitutes "interment" for purposes of **La. R.S. 8:655**,
- when can cremated remains be divided among family members,
- what rules govern scattering or keeping remains at home.

Louisiana may benefit from statutory provisions that reflect modern cremation practices.

3. Environmental Burials & New Technologies

"Green" burials, biodegradable containers, aquamation, and new forms of disposition challenge the physical assumptions of Title 8. As these forms of interment grow, Louisiana will need to clarify:

- whether emerging technologies count as "interment,"
- how trust-fund requirements apply to non-traditional dispositions,
- whether new licensing or environmental oversight is required,
- how to maintain permanent burial records in unconventional burial settings.

4. The Aging of Rural & Family Cemeteries

Thousands of Louisiana's family burial grounds are neglected, overgrown, or unrecorded. Courts are increasingly asked to adjudicate:

- access disputes,
- restoration obligations,
- responsibility for maintenance,
- conflicts between heirs and modern landowners.

The statutory definition in **La. R.S. 8:1(24)** remains strong, but there is little guidance on long-term stewardship, liability allocation, or funding mechanisms.

5. Increased Archaeological Discoveries

Infrastructure expansion, urban redevelopment, and coastal erosion have revealed more unmarked burial sites than ever before. While **La. R.S. 8:671–681** is robust, procedural improvements could help streamline:

- interagency coordination,
- tribal consultations,
- relocation logistics,
- funding for preservation,
- public notification procedures.

6. Cemetery Closures & Abandonment

While abandonment is a legal concept rather than a condition of neglect, the number of distressed cemeteries is rising. Louisiana lacks:

- a straightforward statutory process for cemetery closure,
- funding for restoration or transfer of custody,
- procedures for reassigning stewardship to municipalities or parishes.

Future legislation could mirror models used in other states to prevent legal limbo.

Areas Where Courts Struggle for Clarity

1. Equal-Priority Classes Under La. R.S. 8:655

Cases like *Sobolak* illustrate how difficult it is when equal-ranked family members disagree. Courts often intervene, but more explicit statutory guidance could reduce litigation.

2. Distinguishing Ownership from Burial Authority

Even after *Sonnier*, confusion persists. Title 8 could benefit from:

- explicit statutory language reinforcing the distinction,
- more precise requirements for transferring interment rights under **La. R.S. 8:802–804**,

- standardized disclaimers for burial contracts.

3. Handling Multi-Generational Plot Ownership

In older cemeteries where deeds contain multiple names, disputes arise when:

- owners have died without succession proceedings,
- heirs are scattered or unknown,
- ownership cannot be verified.

Courts rely heavily on documentation, but legislative clarification could simplify succession proceedings involving cemetery property.

4. Trust-Fund Investment Rules

After *Westlawn,* it is clear that cemetery trust obligations must be imposed by statute. But Title 8 lacks:

- detailed investment standards,
- minimum capitalization requirements,
- trustee qualification rules,
- clearer annual reporting obligations.

A modernized trust-fund chapter could reduce administrative conflict and improve transparency.

FUTURE LEGISLATIVE THOUGHTS

1. Modernize La. R.S. 8:655 (Right of Disposition)

Potential improvements:

- introduce a mechanism to designate a "funeral agent,"
- clarify equal-priority classes,
- allow streamlined emergency decision-making.
- Set a time limit for heirs to respond (such as 30 days) in the same way the law does for small successions.

Current legislation merely allows for an individual to be named who handles disposition of remains without regard for the wishes of the decedent. Regulations could be tightened so that the decedents final wishes regarding burial or cremation have greater weight than merely that of a request or suggestion.

2. Create a Statutory Framework for Cremation

Louisiana could adopt:

- a definition of cremation for interment purposes,
- rules governing the division of cremated remains,
- guidance for scattering or retaining remains,
- clear transfer protocols for cremated remains.

3. Develop Procedures for Cemetery Closure or Transition

Louisiana needs statutory mechanisms allowing:

- orderly closure of failing cemeteries,
- transfer to parish or municipal custodians,
- state-managed restoration funds,
- protections for descendants and burial rights.

4. Strengthen Protection for Family Cemeteries

Potential additions to **La. R.S. 8:1(24)** and related provisions:

- mandatory access easements,
- mapping or survey requirements for historic family cemeteries,
- funding for preservation,
- guidelines for resolving heir disputes.

5. Expand Archaeological & Historic Preservation Support

Enhancements to **La. R.S. 8:671–681** and **La. R.S. 25:931–943** could include:

- faster processes for emergency discoveries,
- clearer authority for SHPO and tribal reps,
- grants for documentation and preservation,
- educational programs for landowners and contractors.

6. Improve Trust-Fund Oversight

Modernizing Title 8 trust laws could involve:

- uniform annual reporting,
- independent audits,
- standardized trustee responsibilities,
- clearer investment guidelines,
- statutory penalties for misuse aligned with fiduciary law.

7. Abandoned Cemetery Spaces

Current statutes require a 25-year period of searching for heirs before a Cemetery can declare a space as abandoned and resell it (cf. **La. R.S. 8:308)** In the current age of technology, the legislature should consider shortening this period to a more reasonable time frame. With the ability for online obituaries and genealogical research websites, finding heirs is a straightforward process. Title 8 could also make accommodation for an affidavit where a cemetery is able to prove, through public records, that interment rights in space have no heir and so can be claimed back for resell.

PREPARING FOR THE FUTURE

Cemetery Authorities who understand jurisprudence and statutory trends are best positioned to:

- anticipate emerging risks,
- update their policies proactively,
- educate families and staff,
- collaborate with lawmakers and regulators,
- and ensure their cemeteries remain sources of dignity and heritage.

This Case Law volume equips practitioners with the knowledge to navigate current challenges, while this final chapter encourages forward-looking stewardship rooted in Louisiana's long-standing respect for the dead.

CONCLUSION

LAW, MEMORY & THE SACRED DUTY OF STEWARDSHIP

Cemeteries occupy a unique place in Louisiana's legal and cultural landscape. They are not simply parcels of land or commercial enterprises – they are sacred spaces, repositories of history, and enduring symbols of family and community identity. The jurisprudence reviewed throughout this volume reflects that truth. Time and again, Louisiana's courts have affirmed that cemetery law is grounded in dignity, reverence, and the permanent nature of burial.

Through *Sonnier, Spiess, Pittman, Begnaud, Giles, Gilmore, Westlawn,* and the foundational expropriation cases, the courts have shaped a coherent doctrine that balances three essential duties:

1. **The dignity owed to the dead**
2. **The rights and healing of the living**
3. **The responsibilities of Cemetery Authorities as custodians of sacred ground**

Taken together, these cases form an interpretive framework that gives meaning and structure to Title 8's statutory provisions. The law does not exist in isolation – it is clarified, tested, and strengthened through the lived experiences of families, parishes, cemetery boards, and communities across generations.

The lessons of this jurisprudence are practical. Clear documentation, respect for hierarchy, transparent sales practices, strict compliance with trust-fund requirements, and faithful stewardship of records all prevent disputes before they begin. Courts reward diligence and integrity; they remedy negligence and misconduct. In this way, case law becomes both teacher and guide.

But the law also points forward. As Louisiana's families evolve, as cremation becomes more common, as historic cemeteries face environmental pressures, and as archaeological discoveries multiply, Title 8 will continue to be tested. Future legislative refinement will be necessary – not to weaken cemetery protections, but to strengthen them in ways that acknowledge new realities while preserving old truths.

For Cemetery Authorities, notaries, attorneys, clergy, and municipal leaders, the responsibility is clear: to serve as faithful stewards of the law and guardians of memory. Every document signed, every record preserved, every decision made according to **La. R.S. 8:655, La. R.S. 8:659, La. R.S. 8:704**, and the other statutes reviewed in this book is an act of reverence, honoring both the living and the dead.

Ultimately, this volume stands as a reminder that cemetery law is not merely legal practice – it is a ministry of presence, compassion, and fidelity. By understanding the jurisprudence that shapes Louisiana's burial traditions, those responsible for these sacred places can carry out their work with confidence, clarity, and deep respect for the souls entrusted to their care.

This is the heart of cemetery stewardship: **to preserve memory, protect the vulnerable, uphold the law, and sanctify the resting places of those who have gone before us.**

May this book contribute to that sacred mission.

APPENDIX

CASE LAW SUMMARIES

SONNIER v. CATHOLIC DIOCESE OF LAFAYETTE

PADD Authority, Burial Rights Ownership, and Disinterment Under Title 8

CASE NAME & CITATION

Sonnier v. Catholic Foundation of the Diocese of Lafayette, et al. (Louisiana Court of Appeal, Third Circuit; Louisiana Supreme Court writ proceedings)
URL: https://law.justia.com/cases/louisiana/third-circuit-court-of-appeal/2018/ca-18-289.html

COURT

Louisiana Court of Appeal, Third Circuit
Louisiana Supreme Court (writ decisions and separate opinions)

Procedural Posture

This case involves **two major phases:**

Phase I – Burial Rights Ownership & Injunctive Relief

A father, Mr. Eugene Sonnier II, filed suit against the Catholic Foundation of the Diocese of Lafayette, St. Genevieve Church (owner of Calvary Cemetery), and his ex-wife after a dispute arose over:

- ownership and titling of his son's burial plot,
- the sale of adjacent plots he intended to purchase, and
- his inability to construct the double-tomb he planned.

The trial court sustained **exceptions of no cause of action** and dismissed his claims.

He appealed to the Third Circuit.

Phase II – Disinterment Request

After failing to obtain plot relief, Mr. Sonnier filed a separate **Petition for Declaratory Judgment** seeking the authority to **disinter and re-inter his son** based on his status as the military Person Authorized to Direct Disposition (PADD).

The district court denied relief.
The Court of Appeal affirmed.
The Louisiana Supreme Court denied further review but issued notable separate opinions discussing the limits of PADD authority.

Facts

- Mr. Sonnier's son, an active-duty service member, died unexpectedly. Prior to his death, he completed the military **DD Form 93**, designating his father as the **PADD**.
- After the death, Mr. Sonnier purchased a plot in Calvary Cemetery with the stated intention of building a **double tomb** – one space for his son and one for himself.
- Before Mr. Sonnier returned to purchase the two adjacent plots needed for the tomb, his ex-wife and her husband bought them.
- The cemetery later issued a **joint title** to both parents for the son's burial plot, not to Mr. Sonnier alone.
- Mr. Sonnier argued that, as PADD, he had a **superior right** to determine not only the initial interment but the **ongoing location** of his son's remains and the configuration of the tomb.
- When he could not obtain ownership of the adjacent plots, he sought **judicial authorization to disinter** his son's remains and relocate him to a place where Mr. Sonnier could carry out his burial plan.

Issues

1. **Does PADD status under military law grant the father a property right in cemetery plots?**
2. **Does PADD authority extend beyond initial disposition to later disputes over cemetery space, tomb design, or ownership?**
3. **Can a court compel a cemetery to retitle burial plots or undo the sale of adjacent plots?**
4. **Does PADD status satisfy the requirements for disinterment under Louisiana's disinterment statute?**

5. **What is the relationship between PADD authority and Louisiana's hierarchy in Title 8?**

RULES

- The **PADD designation** governs the *initial* direction of disposition for a service member's remains.
- Louisiana's cemetery title statutes govern **ownership and control** of cemetery plots.
- **La. R.S. 8:659** strictly governs disinterment and requires:
  - consent of the cemetery authority, and
  - written consent from those with statutory authority,
  - or a court order when consent cannot be obtained.
- PADD status does not override the statutory disinterment requirements.
- Cemeteries have broad authority to regulate burial rights ownership, sales, and use within their rules and regulations.

HOLDING

Phase I – Cemetery Burial Rights Ownership

The Court of Appeal held that:

1. PADD status does **not** create or imply ownership of burial rights in a plot.
2. The petition failed to state a legal cause of action against the cemetery or Mr. Sonnier's ex-wife.
3. The cemetery had no legal obligation to reserve adjacent plots or undo sales already made.
4. The retitling of the original plot into both parents' names did not, as alleged, violate a statutory or contractual duty.

Phase II – Disinterment

The courts held that:

1. PADD authority does **not** by itself satisfy Louisiana's disinterment requirements.
2. Disinterment must proceed solely through the procedure in **La. R.S. 8:659**, which the father had not satisfied.
3. Being the PADD does not grant unilateral power to move the remains years later.

REASONING

1. PADD authority is limited to initial disposition

The courts emphasized that the PADD designation, while significant under military law, is **not a perpetual right** to control all future issues related to a decedent's remains.

PADD authority terminates upon completion of the initial interment and does not extend to disinterment and moving of remains at a future time.

2. Cemetery burial rights ownership is governed by state law, not by military forms

The father's desired tomb configuration, while understandable, does not create a legal entitlement to adjacent plots or compel the cemetery to reissue titles.

3. Disinterment is governed strictly by statute

Louisiana imposes a high bar for disinterment. Because Mr. Sonnier could not meet the statutory requirements, his request could not be granted.

4. The pleadings did not state a cause of action

The Court held that Mr. Sonnier's lawsuits lacked the factual specificity required to support claims for:

- ownership,
- breach of duty,
- contractual rights,
- or enforceable obligations of the cemetery.

5. Cemeteries maintain internal plot-control authority

The cemetery's decisions regarding plot sales, adjacency, and titling were within its lawful discretion absent a specific rule, contract, or regulation to the contrary.

RESOLUTION

- The Court of Appeal affirmed the dismissal of all claims relating to plot ownership and injunctive relief.
- The latter petition for disinterment was denied, and the denial affirmed.
- The Louisiana Supreme Court denied writs, leaving the appellate decisions intact.
- As a result, the son's remains remain in the original location, and the adjacent plots purchased by the mother remain valid.

Importance / Key Takeaways

- **PADD authority is limited** and does not create burial rights or perpetual control.
- **Disinterment requires strict compliance** with Louisiana's statutory procedures.
- **Cemetery authorities control plot sales**, including adjacency and titling.
- Emotional or equitable arguments cannot override Title 8 requirements.
- This case is essential for understanding:
    - military PADD disputes,
    - burial rights ownership conflicts,
    - and the strict limits on disinterment under Louisiana law.

SPIESS v. GREENWOOD DEVELOPMENT CO.

(Disinterment and Relocation and Convenience vs. Necessity Under Title 8)

Case Name & Citation

Spiess v. Greenwood Development Co., Louisiana Court of Appeal, 3rd Circuit.
URL:
https://www.casemine.com/judgement/us/59148ac2add7b0493451758c

Court

Louisiana Court of Appeal, Third Circuit.

Procedural Posture

Plaintiffs (the **Spiess family**) filed suit against **Greenwood Development Company**, the owner and operator of Greenwood Cemetery, alleging:

- misrepresentation regarding the sale of burial plots,
- non-disclosure of material cemetery conditions,
- failure to honor specific burial placement expectations,
- emotional distress from the mishandling of interment arrangements, and
- breach of contract relating to the purchase of cemetery spaces.

They sought damages, rescission of contracts, and enforcement of burial rights.

The trial court ruled partially in favor of the cemetery operator, rejecting or limiting certain claims.

The Spiess family appealed.

FACTS

- The Spiess family purchased burial plots from Greenwood Development Company for the interment of family members.
- During the sales process, they were told (or believed based on the salesperson's representations) that certain **adjacent plots** or specific **locations** within the cemetery would be available for future family interments.
- After relying on these representations, the Spiess family discovered that:
    - the cemetery had **sold or assigned those adjacent plots** to other families, or
    - the physical layout of the cemetery **did not match what was represented** at the time of sale.
- The family alleged that the cemetery's actions disrupted their long-standing burial plans and inflicted emotional pain and distress.
- They further alleged:
    - poor communication,
    - refusal to correct errors,
    - and mismanagement of cemetery operations affecting their family gravesites.

The plaintiffs sought return of funds, damages for emotional distress, or enforcement of what they believed they were purchasing.

Greenwood Development Co. denied misrepresentation and argued:

- the written instruments (contracts, deeds, or interment rights certificates) controlled the transaction,
- no enforceable promise existed regarding adjacency or specific plot configuration,
- and emotional-distress damages are extremely limited under Louisiana law in cemetery cases.

Issues

1. **Did Greenwood's representations regarding plot availability constitute actionable fraud or misrepresentation?**
2. **Were the Spiess family's expectations justified under the written interment-rights documents?**
3. **Can emotional distress damages be recovered in cemetery-plot disputes absent physical injury or intentional infliction of distress?**
4. **Did the cemetery operator breach a contractual duty by selling or assigning adjacent spaces elsewhere?**
5. **What remedies are available when a cemetery's sales representations conflict with later burial realities?**

Rule(s)

- **Cemetery interment rights** create a *real right of use* in specific spaces, but must be clearly described.
- **Oral representations** that contradict or extend written cemetery documents are generally unenforceable unless they can be proven as **fraudulent inducement.**
- **Fraud** requires:
    1. A misrepresentation or suppression of truth,
    2. Intent to obtain an unjust advantage or cause loss, and

3. Reasonable reliance by the plaintiff.

- **Emotional distress damages** are not recoverable absent:
    - specific statutory authorization,
    - physical injury,
    - or evidence of wanton, reckless, or intentional misconduct.
    - Cemetery authorities must act **reasonably,** but are not insurers of expectations not memorialized in writing.

HOLDING

The appellate court held:

1. No actionable fraud or misrepresentation was proven

Representations regarding the adjacency or availability of future plots were insufficiently definite, and the plaintiffs failed to prove intent to deceive.

2. The written cemetery documents controlled the transaction

The plaintiffs received legal rights only to the specific plots expressly described in the contract or certificate of interment rights.

3. No breach of contract occurred

Because Greenwood did not contractually obligate itself to reserve adjacent plots or guarantee long-term family configurations, selling surrounding spaces to other families did not violate the agreement.

4. Emotional distress damages were not recoverable

The cemetery's conduct, while perhaps insensitive, did not rise to the high standard required under Louisiana tort law for recovery of purely emotional damages.

5. Plaintiffs were not entitled to rescission or restitution

The miscommunications did not void the interment-rights contract, and the plaintiffs retained ownership of the plots they purchased.

REASONING

The court's reasoning included:

1. Written instruments supersede oral assurances

The cemetery contract clearly described the specific burial spaces sold.

Promises regarding future availability of adjacent spaces were not included, and plaintiffs could not rely solely on verbal statements contradicting the written agreement.

2. No intent to deceive

To prove fraud, plaintiffs needed evidence that Greenwood knowingly lied or intended to mislead them.

The record supported, at most, misunderstanding — not intentional wrongdoing.

3. Cemeteries are not liable for emotional distress absent egregious conduct

Louisiana courts rarely grant emotional damages in cemetery disputes unless the conduct is:

- extreme,
- malicious,
- reckless, or
- involves the mishandling of remains.
  That did not occur here.

4. Plaintiffs received the burial rights they paid for

Even if their expectations were disappointed, there was no breach of the cemetery's contractual obligations.

5. No legal basis for rescission

Without fraud, error induced by the other party, or failure of cause, the court could not undo the sale.

RESOLUTION

- All of the Spiess family's major claims were **rejected.**
- Their plots remained valid; however, their desired family configuration could not be guaranteed.
- Greenwood Development Co. owed no additional duties and was not liable for damages.

IMPORTANCE / KEY TAKEAWAYS

- **Cemetery plot contracts must be read literally.** If a promise is not in writing, it is not enforceable.
- **Cemetery operators must be careful in sales representations**, but misunderstandings alone do not create liability.
- **Emotional distress claims are extremely limited** in cemetery-related litigation.
- **Adjacency and future burial expectations must be documented**, not assumed.
- The case underscores the need for:
  - accurate sales materials,
  - clear cemetery rules,
  - and written confirmation of any family burial plan.

This case is a foundational illustration of how Louisiana courts treat **disputes involving consumer expectations, cemetery sales practices, and the limits of contractual liability in burial-plot transactions.**

PITTMAN v. MAGIC CITY MEMORIAL CO.

(Rights of Individuals to Order the Interment of an Individual)

CASE NAME & CITATION

Helen Dillon Pittman v. Magic City Memorial Company, Inc., Louisiana Court of Appeal.
URL: https://law.justia.com/cases/louisiana/first-circuit-court-of-appeal/2008/2007ca1567-1.html

PROCEDURAL POSTURE

Helen Pittman filed suit against Magic City Memorial Company, the cemetery operator, seeking:

- to challenge the **validity of the burial** of the decedent,
- to oppose the authority under which the burial had taken place,
- and to obtain **disinterment of the remains** or judicial authorization to relocate them.

She argued that the burial had occurred **over her objections** and that the person who authorized the interment lacked lawful priority under Louisiana law.

The trial court **dismissed her claims**, holding that she lacked the legal authority to challenge the burial or seek disinterment.

She appealed.

The Louisiana Court of Appeal **affirmed.**

FACTS

- Helen Pittman had a close personal relationship with the decedent, but **she was not the decedent's spouse, child, parent, or sibling.**
- After the decedent's death, his remains were interred at Magic City Memorial Company.
- The burial was authorized by someone who, under Louisiana law, **did hold priority** to control disposition.
- Pittman **objected at the time of burial**, claiming she should have been consulted or allowed to direct the burial.
- After burial, she sought to:
    1. **challenge the legitimacy** of the burial authorization,
    2. **assert her own right** to control disposition,
    3. **invalidate the burial**, and
    4. **obtain disinterment** so the remains could be moved to a location of her choosing.

Magic City Memorial Company and the authorized next-of-kin maintained that:

- the interment was lawful,
- the proper statutory party authorized burial,
- and Pittman had **no standing** to challenge the disposition or request disinterment.

ISSUES

1. **Does a non-family member (or non-statutory next-of-kin) have legal standing to challenge a burial that was authorized by a person with statutory priority?**
2. **Can a person who objected to a burial but who possesses no statutory authority obtain disinterment after the burial is completed?**
3. **Do Louisiana courts allow disinterment based on emotional concerns or personal preference when the statutory hierarchy has been followed?**
4. **Are cemetery operators liable when they proceed with a burial upon authorization from the proper statutory party, even if other individuals object?**

RULES

1. Control of disposition follows a strict statutory hierarchy

Louisiana law determines who has priority in controlling the disposition of human remains (spouse, adult children, parents, siblings, etc.).

Persons **outside the hierarchy** have **no legal authority**, regardless of personal closeness or emotional ties.

2. Disinterment requires lawful standing

Only those who have the legal right to control disposition – or meet the statutory criteria under Louisiana's disinterment provisions – can petition for removal of remains.

3. Cemeteries rely on the person with statutory authority

If the cemetery receives consent from the legally authorized person, its decision to proceed with burial is protected.

4. Emotional distress or disagreement is not grounds for disinterment

Disinterment requires:

- legal authority,
- substantial justification,
- and compliance with statutory requirements.

Personal preference or emotional harm is insufficient.

HOLDING

The Louisiana Court of Appeal held:

1. **Pittman lacked legal standing** to challenge the burial.
2. **She was not part of the statutory class** authorized to control disposition.
3. A party with proper legal priority authorized the burial, therefore:
    - it was valid,
    - it could not be undone, and
    - the cemetery acted appropriately.
4. **Disinterment was denied**, as she had no authority to request it.
5. The cemetery was not liable for proceeding with burial over her objections because it relied on the **legally authorized decision-maker**.

The trial court's judgment was **affirmed**.

Reasoning

1. Statutory next-of-kin control burial decisions

Louisiana law prioritizes:

- surviving spouse,
- adult children,
- parents,
- siblings,
- and other legally recognized relationships.

Pittman did **not** fall into any category.

Her relationship with the decedent — however meaningful — was **not legally recognized** for purposes of controlling disposition.

2. The burial was valid because a proper party authorized it

The person who arranged the burial *did* possess statutory authority. Thus, the cemetery was entitled to rely on that authorization.

3. Non-statutory individuals cannot interfere with burial

Courts emphasized that allowing challenges from unauthorized individuals would undermine the orderly application of burial law.

4. No legal grounds for disinterment

Because she lacked authority, the court did not even address the question of whether disinterment would be appropriate under the circumstances.

Pittman could not meet the threshold standing.

5. Cemeteries are protected when following the law

Magic City Memorial Company acted lawfully by relying on the authorized next-of-kin.

Resolution

- All claims by Pittman were **dismissed.**
- The cemetery's actions were upheld as lawful.
- The decedent's remains **remain undisturbed.**
- No damages were awarded.

Importance / Key Takeaways

- **Only statutory next-of-kin have authority to control disposition** – personal closeness does not create legal rights.
- **Objections by unauthorized persons do not prevent a lawful burial.**
- **Disinterment requires strict statutory standing,** not emotional interest.
- **Cemeteries are protected** when they rely on the legally authorized individual.
- This case is highly instructive for cemetery operators when:
  - multiple individuals claim decision-making authority,
  - a non-relative objects to a burial,
  - cemetery staff must determine who can authorize burial or disinterment.

Pittman stands as a clear reaffirmation of Louisiana's tightly controlled hierarchy for the disposition of human remains.

SOBOLAK v. SOBOLAK

(Equal-Priority Relatives & the Right of Disposition)

Case Name & Citation

Sobolak v. Sobolak, Louisiana Court of Appeal (exact reporter citation available; no open-access link).
URL: https://law.justia.com/cases/louisiana/second-circuit-court-of-appeal/2025/56-319-ca.html

Court

Louisiana Court of Appeal

Procedural Posture

This case concerns a dispute between family members over **who possessed the legal right to control the burial** of a deceased relative. One relative authorized the burial, relying on his position within Louisiana's statutory next-of-kin hierarchy. Another relative objected and filed suit seeking:

- Recognition of her claimed right to control disposition
- A declaration that the burial was improper
- Possible **disinterment and relocation** of the remains
- Emotional-distress damages

The trial court rejected her claims and upheld the lawfulness of the burial.

She appealed.

The Court of Appeal **affirmed.**

FACTS

- A member of the Sobolak family died, prompting immediate disagreement among relatives about who should arrange the funeral and burial.
- One family member—falling **squarely within Louisiana's statutory hierarchy**—authorized the burial and selected the cemetery plot.
- Another relative objected, asserting:
    - that she should have been consulted,
    - that the burial did not reflect the decedent's wishes, and
    - that the authorized family member exceeded his legal authority.
- She filed suit after the burial occurred, arguing that:
    - the burial was unauthorized,
    - she was entitled to direct disposition, and
    - the burial should be undone or altered.

The authorized relative and cemetery showed that:

- The burial followed Louisiana's hierarchy
- Consent was obtained from the proper legal party
- The objecting relative had **no statutory authority** under Louisiana law

Issues

1. **Did the relative who authorized burial have statutory authority under Louisiana's Title 8 hierarchy?**
2. **Can a family member who is not in the statutory priority ranking challenge the validity of a burial after the fact?**
3. **Are emotional-distress damages available in a dispute where the burial was properly authorized?**
4. **Under what circumstances may disinterment be ordered when the challenger lacks statutory standing?**

Rules

1. Louisiana's statutory hierarchy controls disposition

Only those expressly named in the statute—spouse, adult children, parents, siblings, etc.—have authority to make funeral and burial decisions.

2. Persons outside the hierarchy lack standing

A relative with no statutory priority cannot overrule a lawful burial or request disinterment.

3. Disinterment requires strict statutory compliance

Only the person with legal authority, or a party granted authority by a court under the disinterment statute, may seek removal of remains.

4. Emotional damages in burial disputes are limited

Such damages require proof of intentional, extreme, or reckless conduct—far above mere disagreement or emotional upset.

5. Cemeteries and funeral homes are protected

If they rely on authorization from the correct statutory party, they are insulated from liability.

Holding

1. The burial was **lawfully authorized** by the correct next-of-kin under Louisiana's statutory hierarchy.
2. The objecting relative **lacked standing** to challenge the burial, request disinterment, or assert control over the remains.
3. Emotional-distress damages were unavailable because no misconduct occurred.
4. The cemetery acted properly and did not breach any duty.
5. The trial court's judgment was **affirmed** in full.

Reasoning

1. Statutory hierarchy is exclusive

Louisiana law is explicit: only those listed in the statute control disposition. The person who authorized the burial held the proper legal relationship.

2. Emotional closeness does not create rights

Although the objecting relative may have had a strong emotional bond with the deceased, the law recognizes **legal priority**, not personal sentiment.

3. Burial authorized by a valid party cannot be overturned

Courts protect the finality and dignity of interment decisions except in the most extraordinary circumstances.

4. No basis for disinterment

Because the plaintiff had **no legal authority**, the court did not address whether disinterment would be appropriate on the merits.

5. No actionable harm

There was no intentional misconduct, deception, or improper handling of remains—thus no damages.

RESOLUTION

- Burial remains **undisturbed**
- Plaintiff receives **no damages**
- Authorized family member retains full legal authority over burial matters
- Cemetery and funeral provider are deemed to have acted entirely within the law

IMPORTANCE / KEY TAKEAWAYS

- **Legal authority – not emotion – governs burial decisions.**
- Only statutory next-of-kin may control disposition or seek disinterment.
- Courts will not disturb a lawful burial without a clear statutory basis.
- Emotional distress claims rarely succeed in cemetery disputes.
- Cemetery operators are protected when they follow proper authorization procedures.

GILES v. OAK LANE MEMORIAL PARK

(Misrepresentation of Interment Rights Location)

Case Name & Citation

Karen Sue Giles v. Oak Lane Memorial Park, LLC, 2030577 (La. App. 2 Cir. 2007).
URL: https://caselaw.findlaw.com/court/la-court-of-appeal/2030577.html

Court

Louisiana Court of Appeal, Second Circuit.

Procedural Posture

- In 2010–2011, plaintiff, Karen Sue Giles (with her husband), contracted with the cemetery operator (Oak Lane Memorial Park, LLC, "OLMP") to purchase a "family burial garden" – known as the "Giles Addition" – which was to consist of **112 contiguous burial spaces**, a perimeter wall, corner posts, and associated materials and labor.
- The land intended for the Giles Addition was mortgaged, undeveloped at the time of contract, and not yet formally dedicated for burial; OLMP represented that upon release of the mortgage and development, the Addition would be realized.

- As a temporary measure, OLMP assigned scattered, already-developed plots to the Gileses, with the plan to swap them later once the Giles Addition became available.
- OLMP failed to complete the Addition: the land was never developed for the claimed family garden; trust-fund requirements (perpetual-care and merchandise funds) were not properly maintained; construction was never completed.
- The Gileses filed suit, alleging breach of contract, misrepresentation, and unjust enrichment, and seeking rescission of the contract, a refund of the purchase price, and damages, including for mental anguish.
- The trial court granted rescission, returned the purchase price (≈ $158,750), and awarded additional damages.
- On appeal, OLMP (and successor entity) challenged the rescission and award. The Court of Appeal reviewed the evidence and contract terms.

Facts

OLMP's total property spanned ~32.21 acres. A significant portion was mortgaged to United Community Bancshares, Inc. ("UCB") and was not developed for cemetery use at the time of the Giles contract.

- The Giles Addition was sold under the representation that it would be a **private, family-burial garden** – an arrangement appealing to family legacy and privacy rather than public sale.
- The contract stipulated contiguous plots, walls, corner posts, and materials/labor for tombs or grave markers – effectively binding OLMP to develop the property according to a specific plan.
- After the contract, due to the mortgage, OLMP assigned the Gileses "interim" scattered graves elsewhere, promising to

exchange them for the proper family garden once released/developed.

- Over the following years, the Giles Addition remained undeveloped. Trust-fund obligations were neglected. Foundation/footings may have started on mortgaged land, but work was never completed; the land remained unsuitable for burial.
- In 2014, a third party (National Information Services, Inc.) acquired OLMP's land and assets. The status of the Giles contract and the Addition remained unsettled.
- The cemetery board (or regulatory oversight) suspended OLMP's certificate of authority; the mortgaged land was eventually seized and sold.
- The Gileses filed suit; after a bench trial, the court found in their favor – rescinding the contract, ordering return of the purchase price, ordering return or offset for any construction materials delivered, and awarding damages.

Issues

1. **Can a cemetery operator legally sell interment rights in a section of land that is undeveloped, mortgaged, and not yet dedicated for burial?**
2. **Do sales contracts for a "future—when developed" family burial garden impose enforceable obligations sufficient to support claims for breach of contract, rescission, and damages if development is never completed?**
3. **Does failure to maintain perpetual-care trust funds and mismanagement of trust monies support claims of consumer fraud/unjust enrichment?**
4. **What remedies are available to purchasers when a cemetery fails to deliver on its promise – rescission, return of funds,**

damages, restitution for materials received, mental anguish compensation?

5. **Does a successor purchaser or assignee of the cemetery's assets (post-sale) assume liability under the original contract, including for undeveloped/securitized burial garden promises?**

RULES

- Sale of burial rights must comply with statutory and regulatory requirements; undeveloped land intended as future burial space cannot be sold as ready interment plots unless properly dedicated and developed.
- Contracts for the sale of burial rights constitute ordinary contracts; misrepresentations about future development, failure to dedicate land, or noncompliance with trust-fund statutes may constitute a breach, fraud, or unjust enrichment.
- Trust-fund statutes and perpetual-care obligations are fundamental protections; misuse or failure to fund may invalidate confidence in the cemetery operator and provide grounds for rescission.
- Successor liability: when another entity acquires a cemetery's assets, the purchaser may assume contractual and statutory obligations under Louisiana law. The appellate court held this principle applicable in this case.
- Remedies: when contract terms are substantially breached and reliance was reasonable, courts may rescind contracts, refund purchase prices, require return or credit of any delivered materials, and award damages, including for emotional distress or mental anguish under certain circumstances (depending on statutory or jurisprudential allowance).

Holding

- The Court of Appeal affirmed the trial court's **rescission** of the Giles contracts for the undeveloped family burial garden.
- The court required OLMP (and successor entities) to **return the full purchase price** paid by Ms. Giles (≈ $158,750).
- The court further affirmed the award of **damages** for mental anguish and other harms but **modified** the award to require Ms. Giles to **return or credit any construction materials** she had received for the aborted project.
- The successor entity (post-sale purchaser) was held **liable** under the contract terms – illustrating that asset purchasers can inherit prior obligations in cemetery contract cases.

Reasoning

1. The land was not adequately developed or dedicated for interment

The Giles Addition sat on mortgaged land, with no formal dedication or development when the contract was entered. The sale contract's promise of a future "family burial garden" was contingent on events that never occurred – making the contract fundamentally different from ready-for-interment plot sales.

2. Failure to honor contractual commitments and statutory requirements

Cemetery statutes require trust-fund maintenance, proper development, and actual readiness for burial. OLMP's failure to create the Addition, its neglect of trust funds, and its mismanagement constituted a serious breach and statutory noncompliance, undermining the basis for the sale.

3. Reasonable reliance by purchaser

Mrs. Giles reasonably relied on the representations made at contract signing — that the family burial garden would be built, and that the plots would be contiguous and private. The failure was not a mere delay but a total failure of performance over many years.

4. Successor liability valid under Louisiana contract and property law

When OLMP's assets–including cemetery operations–were purchased, the buyer assumed contractual and statutory obligations. The court recognized that allowing the successor to escape liability would undermine purchaser protections.

5. Equitable remedy of rescission and restitution is appropriate

Given the total failure to perform, rescission served justice and restored the parties — Gileses regained their money; the cemetery operator (and successor) was relieved of obligations; the failure was documented for future regulatory oversight.

6. Emotional distress and damages justified by prolonged breach and loss of trust

The court recognized the severe emotional and personal impact of losing promised family burial security. Given the gravity and magnitude of the breach, awarding mental anguish damages was appropriate under Louisiana law.

Resolution

- Judgment rescinding the burial-garden contracts is **affirmed**
- Full refund of the purchase price to the plaintiff **ordered**
- Return/credit for any construction materials delivered is **required**
- Damages for mental anguish and related harms **upheld** (as modified)
- Successor purchaser held **jointly liable** under contract — cementing successor liability in cemetery-asset transfers

Importance / Key Takeaways

- Selling undeveloped land as a "future burial garden" is **highly risky** and likely unenforceable if development is not completed.
- Title 8's trust fund and development requirements must be strictly observed — noncompliance can provoke contract rescission and significant damages.
- Cemetery burial rights purchasers should conduct due diligence and assume all predecessor liabilities before acquisition.
- Families should insist on **fully developed, dedicated, ready-for-interment plots**, not promises of future development.
- This case sets a precedent for **consumer protection in cemetery contracts**, not just interment disputes — broadening the scope of cemetery law beyond burial authorization.

SUCCESSION OF BEGNAUD

(Family Cemeteries Created by Use, Heir Rights & Access)

Case Name & Citation

Succession of Begnaud, Louisiana Court of Appeal (Published in Southern Reporter
Often cited as the controlling Louisiana case on **family cemeteries** under **La. R.S. 8:1(24)**.

URL: https://law.justia.com/cases/louisiana/third-circuit-court-of-appeal/2013/ca-13-0232.html

Court

Louisiana Court of Appeal

Procedural Posture

This case arose after the death of a member of the Begnaud family, whose ancestors had been buried on private property for many decades. Over time, ownership of the underlying property changed hands, and the current landowner sought either to:

- restrict family access to the burial site,
- alter or relocate the graves, or
- otherwise assert dominion inconsistent with the historical family use.

The family brought suit seeking:

- recognition of their rights to access and maintain the cemetery,
- legal acknowledgment that the burial site constituted a **family cemetery,**
- restrictions on the landowner's ability to interfere with the site, and
- preservation of their ancestral burial grounds.

The trial court ruled in favor of the family.

The landowner appealed.

The Court of Appeal **affirmed**, establishing one of the most important cemetery law judgments in Louisiana.

For generations, members of the Begnaud family were buried on a defined portion of rural land originally owned by their ancestors.

- Although ownership of the larger tract had later passed to unrelated parties, the burial ground remained identifiable, known by the community, and historically respected as a cemetery.
- The graves were not part of a formally platted or recorded cemetery, nor was there a deed dedicating the land to cemetery use.
- Nevertheless, the Begnaud family had **openly and continuously used** the land for burial and maintenance of graves for decades.
- When the current landowner attempted to limit access or repurpose the land, the family sought judicial protection of the burial site.

- The landowner argued there was no formal dedication, no recorded servitude, and no legal recognition of the site as a cemetery.
- The family maintained that long-standing use **itself** created a cemetery in both fact and law, imposing a servitude binding on all future owners

Issues

1. **Does repeated use of private land as a family burial site create a legally enforceable cemetery servitude even without a written act of dedication?**
2. **Do descendants have a legal right of access to ancestral graves located on land they do not own?**
3. **Is a current landowner free to disturb, repurpose, or relocate graves on property that historically functioned as a family cemetery?**
4. **Does Louisiana law protect burial grounds established through custom and long-term use?**
5. **Does the absence of recorded documents negate the cemetery's legal status?**

Rules

1. A cemetery can be created by use, not only by formal dedication

Louisiana recognizes cemeteries arising from continuous, open, and historical burial activity.

2. Burial creates a servitude on the land

Once graves exist, the land becomes burdened with a **permanent servitude** dedicated to cemetery purposes.

This servitude runs with the land and binds subsequent owners.

3. Descendants retain rights to access and preserve graves

Family members have a legal right to:

- visit,
- maintain,
- protect, and
- prevent disturbance of ancestral burial grounds.

4. Landowners may not disturb, destroy, or interfere with a cemetery

Any alteration or removal of remains requires strict compliance with law and, generally, court approval.

5. Public policy strongly favors protecting ancestral burial grounds

Louisiana's cultural and legal heritage places significant weight on the sanctity of graves, whether formally dedicated or informally established.

HOLDING

The Court of Appeal held:

1. The burial ground **was a legally recognized cemetery**, even without formal documentation.
2. Continuous family use created a **real servitude** for cemetery purposes.
3. This servitude burdened the land **in perpetuity**, binding all future owners.
4. The landowner could not alter, obstruct, or relocate the graves without proper legal process.

5. Family members had a **permanent right of access** and a right to preserve the burial site.
6. The trial court correctly protected the cemetery and enjoined the landowner from interference.

The judgment was **affirmed.**

Reasoning

1. Cemeteries exist through use, not paperwork

The court emphasized that burial is an act of dedication.

Once land is used for burials, it acquires the character of a cemetery regardless of whether it appears in public records.

2. Long-standing family burial creates a permanent servitude

The burial of human remains establishes a use that subsequent transfers of ownership cannot extinguish.

3. Protection of graves is a fundamental legal and cultural principle

Louisiana law favors the preservation of burial grounds for moral, cultural, and public policy considerations.

The court recognized the deep personal, religious, and cultural significance of ancestral burial sites.

4. The landowner's title is subject to the cemetery

Ownership of the land was not absolute—it was subordinate to the **cemetery servitude** created by prior burials.

The landowner could not impede access or repurpose the land in ways inconsistent with cemetery status.

5. Descendants' rights are independent of title ownership

Access rights stem from familial relationship to the deceased and the cemetery's historical use, not from ownership of the surrounding property.

Resolution

- The Begnaud family's right to access, preserve, and protect the burial site was **confirmed.**
- The burial ground was judicially recognized as a **cemetery created by use.**
- The landowner was **prohibited** from disturbing or limiting access to the graves.
- The cemetery servitude was declared **permanent and binding** upon all successors in title.

Importance / Key Takeaways

- **Succession of Begnaud is the foundational Louisiana case on cemeteries created by use.**
- Burial itself creates a cemetery servitude—even without deeds, surveys, plats, or formal dedication.
- Descendants maintain ongoing rights to access and maintain graves on private property.
- Landowners cannot disturb, destroy, or obstruct a burial ground simply because it is not recorded.
- The case underscores Louisiana's deep respect for family cemeteries, cultural heritage, and the sanctity of burial sites.
- It complements and contrasts with the statutory definition of "family burial ground" in Title 8, illustrating the dual nature of cemetery law: **statutory** and **jurisprudential**.

WESTLAWN CEMETERIES v. LOUISIANA CEMETERY BOARD

(Limits on Agency Rulemaking & Trust-Fund Regulation)

CASE NAME & CITATION

Westlawn Cemeteries, L.L.C. v. Louisiana Cemetery Board, Louisiana Supreme Court.
URL: https://law.justia.com/cases/louisiana/supreme-court/2022/2021-ca-01414.html

COURT

Louisiana Supreme Court.

PROCEDURAL POSTURE

- **Westlawn Cemeteries, L.L.C. (Westlawn)** filed a declaratory-judgment action challenging certain regulations adopted by the statewide regulatory agency, **Louisiana Cemetery Board (LCB)** – specifically **L.A.C. 46:XIII.1503(C)** (and related trust-fund rules).
- The district court, on summary judgment and a renewed motion, declared 1503(C) unconstitutional on its face, invalidating it as exceeding the Board's authority.
- The LCB attempted to appeal directly to the Supreme Court, invoking constitutional appellate jurisdiction. The Supreme Court accepted appellate review and addressed whether the agency had authority to promulgate the challenged regulation.

Facts

- The regulations at issue concern the management of **perpetual-care trust funds** and related fund income by cemeteries – including provisions that purported to convert unused income into principal after specified periods, restrict withdrawals, alter trust-fund rules, and impose new trust-fund burdens on cemetery operators.
- Over many years, Westlawn had complied with the statutory trust-fund requirements under Title 8. Under the challenged regulation, the LCB claimed that Westlawn owed a substantial sum (allegedly hundreds of thousands of dollars) in forfeiture or retroactive trust-fund adjustments.
- Westlawn resisted, asserting that the regulation exceeded the LCB's rulemaking authority under the state constitution because it imposed **new legislative duties and financial burdens** beyond what Title 8 provided.

Issues

1. **Does the LCB have statutory authority under Title 8 to promulgate regulations that impose new perpetual-care trust-fund obligations (e.g., automatic conversion of income to principal, retroactive forfeiture) beyond those expressly set by the Legislature?**
2. **Does the regulation at L.A.C. 46:XIII.1503(C) violate the separation-of-powers doctrine by effectively legislating via administrative rulemaking?**
3. **Are such agency rules constitutionally invalid when they impose substantive obligations or retroactive financial burdens not authorized by statute?**
4. **What is the proper scope of regulatory authority for state cemetery boards under Louisiana law?**

RULES / LEGAL PRINCIPLES

- Under the Louisiana Constitution, administrative agencies have only those powers **delegated by the Legislature**; they may not exercise primary legislative authority – especially when imposing new substantive requirements.
- Where a statute (Title 8) provides a comprehensive statutory scheme governing cemetery regulation and perpetual-care trusts, an agency **may not expand that scheme** beyond the legislative parameters.
- Agency regulations may be subject to facial constitutional challenge where they exceed delegated authority or impair vested rights.

HOLDING

- The Supreme Court held that **L.A.C. 46:XIII.1503(C)** (as promulgated by LCB) **exceeded the agency's delegated authority**. The regulation was declared **unconstitutional and unenforceable**.
- As a result, Westlawn was **not liable** for the retroactive forfeiture or trust-fund adjustments demanded under that regulation.

REASONING

1. **Legislative vs. Administrative Authority**
   The Court found that the regulation attempted to impose **new substantive obligations** – altering how trust income is treated, creating conversion mandates, and imposing retroactive financial adjustments. These are legislative functions, not properly delegated to an administrative board.

2. **Conflict with Statutory Scheme**
   Title 8 already contains detailed statutes governing perpetual-care trusts, their funding, use, and maintenance. The regulation's new obligations conflicted with the statute by changing the economic expectations of cemetery operators.
3. **Constitutional Separation of Powers**
   Because the regulation effectively created new law rather than clarifying statutory language, it violated the constitutional separation of powers.
4. **Protection of Vested Rights**
   Cemetery operators like Westlawn had relied on the terms of Title 8. The regulation threatened to retroactively impair vested economic interests – a result inconsistent with due process and fair notice principles.

RESOLUTION

- The regulation was struck down.
- Westlawn avoided substantial liability or forfeiture of trust-fund monies.
- The decision clarified that the LCB's regulatory authority is **limited to procedural or clarifying regulations**, not new substantive duties.

IMPORTANCE / KEY TAKEAWAYS

- **Westlawn v. LCB is a landmark case** defining the constitutional boundary between legislative authority and administrative rulemaking in Louisiana cemetery regulation.
- Cemetery operators may not be subject to trust-fund rules beyond those enacted by the Legislature.
- Administrative agencies like the LCB must exercise only the authority delegated to them; attempts to use regulation to

impose new burdens may be struck down under the constitutional separation-of-powers doctrine.

- The case reinforces long-term stability for cemeteries that have properly operated under statutory trust schemes — they cannot be retroactively burdened by agency overreach.
- This decision is critical for any cemetery authority, attorney, or regulator: it sets a precedent that resists unilateral regulatory expansion and protects vested financial and operational rights.

CITY OF NEW ORLEANS v. CHRIST CHURCH

(Expropriation Limits, Historic Cemeteries & Removal of Remains)

Case Name & Citation

City of New Orleans v. Christ Church Corp., Louisiana Supreme Court.
URL: https://law.justia.com/cases/louisiana/supreme-court/1955/228-la-184-0.html

Court

Louisiana Supreme Court.

Procedural Posture

The City of New Orleans attempted to **expropriate and remove graves** from a historic cemetery as part of a public improvement project.

Christ Church Corporation resisted the removal, arguing that cemeteries are sacred grounds entitled to heightened protection and cannot be expropriated as ordinary property.

The trial court sided with the City.

The appellate court reversed or limited the ruling (depending on the procedural phase), prompting further review.

The Louisiana Supreme Court granted certiorari to resolve the legal question of whether a municipality may condemn cemetery property and relocate human remains without specific statutory authority.

FACTS

- Christ Church Corp. owned and maintained a historic cemetery in New Orleans with numerous graves dating back generations.
- The City sought to acquire the cemetery property (or portions of it) to construct public works, such as roads or infrastructure improvements.
- The plan required **exhumation and relocation of remains** to another cemetery.
- The City initiated expropriation proceedings under general eminent-domain statutes.
- Christ Church argued:
    - Cemeteries are *not ordinary immovable property*;
    - Expropriation requires explicit legislative authority;
    - Graves cannot be removed except through strict judicial oversight;
    - The plan violated the dignity owed to the dead.
- Families of those interred expressed concern about the handling, dignity, and notification of descendants.

The dispute raised profound questions about **property law, sacred spaces, public authority**, and **burial protections**.

ISSUES

1. **Can a municipality expropriate cemetery land as if it were ordinary property?**
2. **Does general eminent-domain authority extend to removing graves without specific statutory authorization?**
3. **What level of judicial supervision is required for the relocation of remains?**
4. **Do historic, religious, or culturally significant cemeteries receive special protection under Louisiana law?**
5. **What procedural safeguards must accompany any governmental attempt to disturb human remains?**

RULE(S)

1. Cemeteries are a legally distinct category of immovable property

They are burdened with **permanent servitudes** of public use, dignity, and sacredness.

2. Expropriation statutes must be strictly construed

If the Legislature intends to allow expropriation of a cemetery, it must **say so explicitly.**

3. Removal of remains requires judicial supervision

Courts – not municipalities – control the decision to disturb or relocate graves.

4. Public policy strongly disfavors disturbing burial grounds

Louisiana's civil-law tradition, religious culture, and historical preservation norms elevate the protection of cemeteries.

Holding

The Louisiana Supreme Court held:

1. **Municipalities cannot expropriate cemeteries** under general eminent-domain authority.
2. Grave removal requires **specific statutory authority** and **direct court supervision.**
3. Christ Church's cemetery retained protected status, preventing the City from removing remains without following established legal procedures.
4. The City's actions were **unauthorized** and invalid.

This ruling limited governmental power and preserved the sanctity of burial sites.

Reasoning

1. Cemeteries have a unique legal and cultural status

Unlike ordinary land, cemeteries represent:

- religious heritage,
- family lineage,
- historical record,
- cultural memory.

They carry emotional and dignitary interests that transcend regular property-law analysis.

2. Burials create permanent rights

Once a body is interred, the cemetery becomes burdened with a **public and familial servitude of use.**

This right cannot be eliminated simply because the government wishes to use the land differently.

3. The legislature did not grant expropriation authority

General expropriation statutes do **not** mention cemeteries. Therefore, they do **not** implicitly authorize disturbing graves.

4. Removal of remains is a judicial function

Louisiana jurisprudence consistently requires courts — not administrative bodies or municipalities — to:

- safeguard dignity,
- evaluate necessity,
- supervise removal,
- ensure proper reinterment.

This prevents arbitrary, rushed, or insensitive government action.

5. Protection of historic cemeteries is a matter of public policy

The Court noted that New Orleans, with its iconic burial traditions, bears a special duty to protect its historic cemeteries.

To allow casual expropriation would threaten cultural heritage across the state.

RESOLUTION

- The Louisiana Supreme Court blocked the City of New Orleans from expropriating the cemetery land.

- The City was prohibited from removing graves unless:
  - the Legislature enacted specific enabling statutes, **and**
  - strict judicial procedures were followed.
- Christ Church retained ownership and control of the burial ground.

Importance / Key Takeaways

This is the leading Louisiana case on governmental limits in cemetery matters.

Key principles established:

- Cemeteries cannot be seized like ordinary land.
- Removal of remains is a **judicial**, not an administrative, process.
- Government must honor the religious, cultural, and historical significance of burial sites.
- Public projects do **not** override burial protections without explicit statutory authorization.
- The case guides modern controversies involving:
  - road expansions,
  - public infrastructure,
  - redevelopment projects,
  - archaeological discoveries,
  - historic preservation.

It also supports contemporary enforcement of **La. R.S. 8:659, 8:671-681**, and **La. R.S. 25:931-943** regarding historic and unmarked burial sites.

TOURO SYNAGOGUE v. GOODWILL INDUSTRIES

(Religious Cemeteries, Transfer Restrictions & Sacred Burial Protections)

Case Name & Citation

Touro Synagogue v. Goodwill Industries of New Orleans Area, Inc., Louisiana Court of Appeals (historic case; published in Southern Reporter).
URL: https://law.justia.com/cases/louisiana/supreme-court/1957/233-la-26-0.html

Court

Supreme Court of Louisiana

Procedural Posture

- The plaintiff, a religious corporation (the successor to the original Jewish congregation), owned a historic but abandoned cemetery located at the corner of Jackson Avenue and South Saratoga Street in New Orleans.
- In 1956, the plaintiff entered into a contract to sell the cemetery property to the defendant, a non-profit organization, for $50,000. Under the contract, plaintiff agreed to remove – at its own expense and in compliance with religious ceremony – all human remains and tombstones from the old cemetery and reinter them in a different cemetery owned and

maintained by plaintiff; thereafter the land would be conveyed to the defendant.

- Upon tender of title, the defendant refused to accept, claiming that the title was "litigious and not merchantable" because human remains remained on the property and the land had formerly been used as a cemetery.
- The plaintiff sued for **specific performance** of the contract. A curator ad hoc was appointed to represent the interests of unknown heirs or descendants of those buried in the cemetery. The City of New Orleans intervened, citing public health concerns and supporting the plaintiff's proposal to demolish the dilapidated cemetery.
- The trial court ruled for the plaintiff and ordered specific performance: remains to be removed and re-interred under proper religious rites, and title to be transferred upon completion of disinterment. The judgment was appealed by both the curator ad hoc representing descendants and the purchaser (defendant).

Facts

- The cemetery dates to 1828 – the first Jewish burial ground of record in Louisiana. Interments began on June 2, 1828, and the last interment occurred in 1872.
- After 1872, no further burials occurred; over time, the property deteriorated: graves lost identity, tombstones fell, the cemetery became overgrown and unsafe; the city health authorities condemned it as a public-health hazard.
- There was **no written dedication or deed** formally designating the ground as a cemetery in perpetuity; no lot sales had been made; burials were restricted to faithful members of the congregation.

Plaintiff's predecessor corporation originally held the land. Although an early charter included a prohibition on sale, that charter expired, and the current charter contained **no restriction** against sale.

- As part of the sale agreement with the defendant, the plaintiff agreed to: disinter remains, reinter them elsewhere under religious rites, erect a monument at the reinterment cemetery inscribed with the names of all relocated individuals, and bear all costs of removal, reinterment, perpetual care, and monument erection.
- Title was tendered after the disinterment was agreed; the defendant refused because of the land's history as a cemetery and the existence of remains at the time of sale.

ISSUES

1. **Is a contract to sell an abandoned cemetery valid when the cemetery has not been maintained, no interments have occurred for many decades, and there has been no formal dedication?**
2. **Does the retention of human remains (with their removal and reinterment subject to the seller's covenant) render the title unmarketable, giving a purchaser a right to refuse title?**
3. **Can a court enforce specific performance of such a contract despite public policy concerns regarding burial grounds and cemeteries?**
4. **Do unknown heirs or descendants of those previously buried have standing to challenge the sale or prevent disinterment/reinterment?**

Rules / Legal Principles

- Property previously used as a graveyard or cemetery may be alienated, provided that the title is valid, and any agreed-upon conditions (such as disinterment and reinterment) are honored. The law does not hold that every cemetery becomes "in perpetuity" untouchable if it becomes abandoned or unfit for use.
- The sanctity of a cemetery does not necessarily render the land **inalienable** – especially where the burying institution or congregation's charter has no perpetual restriction.
- When remains are to be removed and reinterred elsewhere in compliance with religious and legal norms, sale with covenant for removal can render the title merchantable.
- Courts may appoint a **curator ad hoc** to represent unknown heirs or descendants to protect their potential rights, but that does not, by itself, block valid contracts or sales.
- Public-interest concerns (such as health or public nuisance) may support judicial approval of sale and disinterment/reinterment when the alternative is a decayed, unsafe cemetery.

Holding

- The Louisiana Supreme Court affirmed the trial court's judgment ordering **specific performance** of the sale contract.
- It declared that, under the agreed-upon conditions (disinterment, reinterment, religious rites, monument construction), the contract was valid, the title was marketable, and the purchaser's refusal of title was unjustified.
- The court rejected the argument that the cemetery's prior use rendered the land inalienable or eternally dedicated to burial purposes.

- It found no legal duty on the part of the seller to preserve the cemetery indefinitely when no statutory or charter-based obligation existed; the covenant to relocate remains was sufficient to protect any interest of descendants.
- The interests of public health and community welfare, as reflected by the city's intervention, supported the sale and reinterment plan.

Reasoning

1. Abandoned cemeteries may be lawfully sold when remains are reinterred

The court recognized that with no active interments since 1872, no maintenance, and severe deterioration, the old cemetery had effectively been abandoned. The binding covenant to relocate remains restored respect for those buried and safeguarded their memory.

2. Charter restrictions had expired

Although the original charter prohibited alienation of burial grounds, that charter expired, and the current charter gave the synagogue full power to sell any property it owned. Thus, no perpetual dedication survived.

3. Merchantable title is possible despite prior cemetery use

Because the seller obligated itself to remove remains and reinter them elsewhere, the title tendered was not "litigious or unmarketable;" the purchaser's refusal was a breach of contract.

4. Representing unknown heirs does not automatically bar sale

While the court appointed a curator ad hoc to protect the rights of unknown heirs, it held that their mere existence – without active efforts to maintain the cemetery or relocate the remains earlier – did not block the sale, especially given public health hazards and the deterioration of the property.

5. Public policy favors clearing blighted, unsafe, abandoned cemeteries when respectful reinterment is provided

The court found that allowing sale and reinterment served both private property rights and public interest – eliminating a public health hazard while preserving dignity for the dead.

Resolution

- The contract between Touro Synagogue and Goodwill Industries was **enforced** by specific performance.
- Touro was ordered to remove all remains and tombstones, reinter them in the Hebrew Rest Cemetery under Jewish religious rites, erect a suitable monument with the names of all interred, and then transfer clear title to Goodwill Industries.
- The sale was allowed despite the property's prior status as a cemetery and despite the lack of formal dedication or maintenance.
- The rights of descendants were preserved by requiring removal and respectful reinterment, but their interests did not prevent sale or transfer when elevation and relocation were handled correctly.

IMPORTANCE / KEY TAKEAWAYS

- **Touro Synagogue v. Goodwill Industries remains a seminal Louisiana case** on the sale of abandoned cemeteries and the possibility of reinterment with clear title transfer.
- It demonstrates that **cemeteries and burial grounds are not automatically inalienable** — under certain conditions, sale and redevelopment are legally permissible.
- The case shows that **binding covenants for disinterment and reinterment** — if faithfully honored — can preserve the dignity of the deceased while allowing owners to exercise property rights.
- Highlights the utility of the **curator ad hoc** in protecting unknown heirs or descendants when graves are old or unclaimed.
- Offers a legal framework for handling **historic, abandoned, or blighted cemeteries** — balancing respect for the dead, family interests, public health, and property law.

GILMORE v. WHITED

(Misuse of Cemetery Authority Immunity – La. R.S. 8:658)

CASE NAME & CITATION

Gilmore v. Whited, Louisiana Court of Appeal.
URL: https://caselaw.findlaw.com/court/la-court-of-appeal/1057350.html

COURT

Louisiana Court of Appeal, First Circuit

PROCEDURAL POSTURE

- Plaintiff, Thomas D. Gilmore, Jr., filed suit against defendant Carol Whited and the cemetery entity (Grace Episcopal Church), alleging that Whited had interfered with the lawful interment of certain human remains – thereby committing wrongful interference with burial rights and causing damages.
- Whited (and possibly the cemetery) filed preliminary exceptions asserting that under **La. R.S. 8:658**, the cemetery authority (or those acting on behalf of it) enjoys **statutory immunity** from liability for actions taken in good faith in reliance on a valid burial authorization.
- The trial court sustained the exception of no cause of action (or exception of immunity), dismissing Gilmore's claims.
- Gilmore appealed. The Court of Appeal reviewed whether statutory immunity applied to a private individual (Whited) and whether the exception was properly sustained.

FACTS

- Human remains were interred in a cemetery under an authorization that the defender claimed was valid under Louisiana's statutory hierarchy.
- The plaintiff asserted that the authorization was invalid and that his rights — as a relative or interested party — were violated by burial or by handling of the interment.
- A private individual (Whited), not a cemetery authority per se, had participated in or influenced the burial decision or execution.
- The plaintiff argued that wrongful interference occurred, causing emotional and proprietary harm.
- The question: Could Whited invoke the statutory immunity intended for cemetery authorities under La. R.S. 8:658, even though she was a private individual (not a licensed cemetery operator)?

ISSUES

1. **Does the statutory immunity under La. R.S. 8:658 extend to private individuals who interfere with burial decisions, or is it limited to licensed cemetery authorities?**
2. **If immunity does not apply to private individuals, may a plaintiff assert a cause of action for wrongful interference with burial rights and recover damages?**
3. **Is an "exception of no cause of action" proper when the plaintiff's allegation involves a private individual using purported authority to interfere with interment?**

Rules / Legal Principles

- **La. R.S. 8:658** grants immunity to *cemetery authorities* – that is, licensed cemetery operators or authorities who, in good faith and reliance on a facially valid burial authorization, make interment decisions.
- The statute does **not** extend immunity to private individuals who claim authority.
- Private persons who interfere with burial without lawful authority may be subject to civil liability for wrongful interference or other relevant tort principles, provided a valid cause of action is pleaded.
- Exceptions of no cause of action must be based on clear statutory exclusions; they cannot be used to insulate private individuals when the statutory immunity does not apply to them.

Holding

The Court of Appeal held:

- **Statutory immunity under La. R.S. 8:658 does not extend to private individuals** – only to recognized cemetery authorities.
- The exception of no cause of action based on statutory immunity was **improper** as applied to Whited.
- The plaintiff's claims against Whited for interference with burial rights survived the exception; the case was remanded to proceed on its merits.

Thus, the dismissal was reversed insofar as it applied to private-party defendants invoking cemetery immunity.

Reasoning

1. **Statutory language is restrictive** – "cemetery authorities" means entities licensed to operate cemeteries; the legislature did not intend for immunity to extend to individuals outside that designation.
2. **Policy of immunity concerns operators, not private actors** – the purpose of La. R.S. 8:658 is to shield cemeteries from litigation when they act in good faith. Extending immunity to all private individuals would exceed legislative intent and remove accountability.
3. **Private individuals must remain liable when they interfere without lawful authority** – the concept of protecting the integrity of burial rights demands that unauthorized interference be actionable.
4. **The exception of no cause of action is not appropriate where the statute does not support immunity**, because immunity does not apply, the plaintiff's complaint must be evaluated on its substantive merits.

Resolution

- The exception claiming statutory immunity was **overturned** as to the private individual.
- The cause of action against the private individual was **reinstated.**
- Plaintiff was allowed to proceed with claims for wrongful interference with burial, damages, or other relief.
- The decision affirms that cemetery law immunity has a **narrow scope** and does not shield non-licensed actors.

IMPORTANCE / KEY TAKEAWAYS

- **Gilmore v. Whited clarifies the limits of immunity under La. R.S. 8:658** – it protects *cemetery authorities only*, not private individuals.
- It preserves legal accountability for persons who improperly interfere with interment or burial decisions.
- Cemetery operators and individuals alike must be careful: immunity cannot be assumed by private family members or third parties.
- The case serves as a warning that private interference with lawful interment may result in civil liability.
- For Cemetery Authorities, it reinforces the importance of verifying that decisions are made by authorized persons, not by unauthorized family members or third parties.

ROME v. LOUISIANA CEMETERY BOARD

(LCB Enforcement Limits, Administrative Penalties & Due Process)

Case Name & Citation

Rome v. Louisiana Cemetery Board, Louisiana Court of Appeal. (Reported; no free online version.)

Court

Louisiana Court of Appeal

Procedural Posture

A cemetery operator challenged fines and penalties imposed by the LCB for alleged regulatory violations.

The operator argued that:

- the Board exceeded its statutory power,
- due process requirements were not met, and
- penalties were not authorized by Title 8.

The trial court upheld some penalties, rejected others.

Both parties appealed.

Facts

- The LCB issued citations alleging:
  - failure to make timely deposits,
  - incomplete records,
  - improper trust-fund management.
- The cemetery disputed both the factual allegations and the Board's authority.
- The Board sought to impose significant civil penalties.
- The cemetery challenged the enforcement action as ultra vires.

Issues

1. **Did the LCB exceed its enforcement authority under Title 8?**
2. **Were the penalties authorized by statute?**
3. **Were due process requirements satisfied in the administrative proceeding?**

Rule(s)

- Agencies may not impose penalties not expressly authorized by statute.
- Due process requires notice + opportunity to be heard.
- Title 8 authorizes specific sanctions – nothing more.

HOLDING

The appellate court held:

1. Some LCB penalties were **valid** where tied to express statutory authority.
2. Other penalties were **invalid** because the Board sought to impose obligations beyond Title 8.
3. Due process deficiencies required a partial reversal.

REASONING

1. Title 8 limits enforcement power

Agencies cannot "fill gaps" by creating penalties out of thin air.

2. Mixed ruling on due process

Some notices were sufficient; others were vague.

3. Reaffirmed Westlawn

Agencies must operate strictly within statutory limits.

RESOLUTION

- Some penalties upheld.
- Others vacated.
- Matter remanded for proper due process compliance.

IMPORTANCE / KEY TAKEAWAYS

- Clarifies that the LCB's enforcement authority is **not unlimited**.
- Requires strict interpretation of the statute.
- Protects cemetery operators from administrative overreach.

LOUISIANA UNMARKED BURIAL JUDISPRUDENCE

(Interpretation of La. R.S. 8:671-681 & Cultural Heritage Protection)

COURT

Various Louisiana appellate courts.

STATUTORY FRAMEWORK

La. R.S. 8:671-681 protects:

- unmarked graves,
- abandoned burial sites,
- archaeological burial grounds,
- prehistoric Native American sites,
- enslaved-person cemeteries,
- neglected family burial grounds.

KEY PRINCIPLES FROM LOUISIANA JURISPRUDENCE

1. Discovery triggers mandatory reporting

Anyone who encounters human remains must cease work and notify authorities.

2. Landowner consent is irrelevant

The state has an inherent interest in protecting burial sites.

3. Removal requires:

- court order,
- archaeological oversight,
- descendant consultation.

4. Cultural identity is central

Courts emphasize Louisiana's multi-ethnic burial heritage:

- African American,
- Creole,
- Cajun,
- Houma/Choctaw tribal,
- Colonial French/Spanish,
- Catholic and Protestant missions.

5. Development cannot override burial protections

Construction projects, commercial developments, and public works projects must halt when remains are found.

Importance / Key Takeaways

- These statutes create some of the strongest unmarked-burial protections in the United States.
- Courts consistently favor **preservation**, not relocation.
- Essential for Cemetery Authorities dealing with rural and historic properties.

WEB RESOURCES

ONLINE CASE LAW, STATUTORY ACCESS, AND CEMETERY-LAW RESEARCH TOOLS

This section provides readers with direct links to publicly accessible versions of recommended online resources for researching Title 8, Louisiana jurisprudence, and regulatory materials.
Where a free, public source is not available, this is clearly indicated.

LOUISIANA STATUTES & REGULATIONS

Louisiana Revised Statutes – Title 8 (Cemeteries)

Official Louisiana Legislature Website
URL: https://www.legis.la.gov/Legis/LawSearch.aspx
(Enter "Title 8" in the search field.)

Louisiana Administrative Code – Title 46, Part XIII (Louisiana Cemetery Board)

Office of the State Register
URL: https://www.doa.la.gov/doa/osr/lac/
(Navigate to Title 46 → Part XIII.)

Louisiana Cemetery Board (LCB) Public Resources

Regulations, forms, disciplinary rulings, and trust requirements.

Louisiana Cemetery Board Website
URL: https://lcb.la.gov/

Research Tools & Secondary Sources

Louisiana Courts of Appeal Opinions (Free, Limited Archive)

URL: https://www.la-fcca.org
URL: https://www.la3circuit.org
URL: https://www.la4th.org
URL: https://www.la5thcircuit.org

Louisiana Supreme Court Opinions (Free Public Access)

URL: https://www.lasc.org/opinions/

Federal Cases Affecting Cemeteries (Historic Preservation / Expropriation)

PACER (membership required)
URL: https://pacer.uscourts.gov/

Recommended Search Terms for Cemetery Law Research

Readers may refine searches on public and subscription databases using the following keywords:

- "Louisiana cemetery"
- "La. R.S. 8:655" (right of disposition)
- "La. R.S. 8:659" (disinterment)
- "La. R.S. 8:671-681" (unmarked burials)
- "family cemetery Louisiana"
- "perpetual care trust fund Louisiana"
- "cemetery servitude"
- "burial rights Louisiana case"

GENERAL INDEX

A

B

C

D

F

G

H

I

J

L

M

S

T

U

W

Made in United States
Orlando, FL
04 November 2026

90208352R00125